DOUBLE & TRIPLE ADDITION AND SUBTRACTION WORKBOOK

DAY 1 Name _____ Score /25

Double Digit Adding - No Regrouping   Date _____

1) 28 + 20	2) 24 + 54	3) 11 + 84	4) 10 + 66	5) 27 + 50
6) 21 + 32	7) 64 + 13	8) 43 + 26	9) 28 + 20	10) 62 + 14
11) 21 + 42	12) 81 + 11	13) 48 + 51	14) 50 + 27	15) 16 + 40
16) 37 + 22	17) 44 + 14	18) 34 + 35	19) 80 + 18	20) 54 + 10
21) 16 + 22	22) 13 + 13	23) 12 + 43	24) 57 + 41	25) 40 + 28

This Book Belongs To:

_____

Table of Contents

Double Digit Adding - No Regrouping

Date _____

1)   28
+ 20

2)   24
+ 54

3)   11
+ 84

4)   10
+ 66

5)   27
+ 50

6)   21
+ 32

7)   64
+ 13

8)   43
+ 26

9)   28
+ 20

10)   62
+ 14

11)   21
+ 42

12)   81
+ 11

13)   48
+ 51

14)   50
+ 27

15)   16
+ 40

16)   37
+ 22

17)   44
+ 14

18)   34
+ 35

19)   80
+ 18

20)   54
+ 10

21)   16
+ 22

22)   13
+ 13

23)   12
+ 43

24)   57
+ 41

25)   40
+ 28

DAY 2

Double Digit Adding - No Regrouping

Date _____

1)   39
+   50
_____

2)   48
+   11
_____

3)   29
+   10
_____

4)   15
+   34
_____

5)   28
+   40
_____

6)   64
+   12
_____

7)   51
+   21
_____

8)   30
+   28
_____

9)   48
+   20
_____

10)   63
+   11
_____

11)   60
+   30
_____

12)   75
+   10
_____

13)   13
+   21
_____

14)   42
+   50
_____

15)   69
+   30
_____

16)   73
+   21
_____

17)   87
+   10
_____

18)   27
+   41
_____

19)   78
+   21
_____

20)   19
+   50
_____

21)   12
+   24
_____

22)   62
+   13
_____

23)   82
+   17
_____

24)   55
+   14
_____

25)   10
+   65
_____

DAY 3

Score /25

Double Digit Adding - No Regrouping

Date _____

1) 48
  + 30

2) 89
  + 10

3) 62
  + 11

4) 67
  + 22

5) 37
  + 22

6) 42
  + 43

7) 79
  + 10

8) 64
  + 33

9) 19
  + 40

10) 57
   + 42

11) 50
   + 45

12) 52
   + 33

13) 43
   + 30

14) 28
   + 50

15) 82
   + 17

16) 11
   + 84

17) 20
   + 51

18) 18
   + 61

19) 87
   + 10

20) 71
   + 10

21) 68
   + 21

22) 38
   + 50

23) 26
   + 63

24) 22
   + 26

25) 12
   + 13

Name _____

Double Digit Adding - No Regrouping

Date _____

1) 47
 + 32
___

2) 25
 + 14
___

3) 56
 + 31
___

4) 88
 + 10
___

5) 52
 + 37
___

6) 80
 + 10
___

7) 37
 + 30
___

8) 58
 + 40
___

9) 37
 + 60
___

10) 31
  + 25
___

11) 73
  + 10
___

12) 52
  + 41
___

13) 70
  + 19
___

14) 66
  + 11
___

15) 16
  + 50
___

16) 81
  + 10
___

17) 57
  + 10
___

18) 65
  + 34
___

19) 77
  + 21
___

20) 43
  + 30
___

21) 82
  + 12
___

22) 26
  + 20
___

23) 38
  + 21
___

24) 15
  + 41
___

25) 34
  + 60
___

DAY 5

Double Digit Adding - No Regrouping   Date _____

1) 70
  + 13

2) 37
  + 12

3) 14
  + 61

4) 65
  + 12

5) 63
  + 26

6) 38
  + 51

7) 31
  + 18

8) 85
  + 11

9) 61
  + 18

10) 67
   + 20

11) 41
   + 22

12) 84
   + 13

13) 78
   + 20

14) 18
   + 31

15) 25
   + 70

16) 80
   + 13

17) 80
   + 15

18) 86
   + 10

19) 61
   + 37

20) 40
   + 29

21) 58
   + 41

22) 15
   + 70

23) 67
   + 30

24) 75
   + 22

25) 62
   + 30

Name _____

Double Digit Adding - No Regrouping

Date _____

1) $\begin{array}{r} 61 \\ +\ 13 \\ \hline \end{array}$
2) $\begin{array}{r} 61 \\ +\ 28 \\ \hline \end{array}$
3) $\begin{array}{r} 45 \\ +\ 32 \\ \hline \end{array}$
4) $\begin{array}{r} 76 \\ +\ 22 \\ \hline \end{array}$
5) $\begin{array}{r} 22 \\ +\ 47 \\ \hline \end{array}$

6) $\begin{array}{r} 84 \\ +\ 12 \\ \hline \end{array}$
7) $\begin{array}{r} 75 \\ +\ 21 \\ \hline \end{array}$
8) $\begin{array}{r} 58 \\ +\ 40 \\ \hline \end{array}$
9) $\begin{array}{r} 28 \\ +\ 50 \\ \hline \end{array}$
10) $\begin{array}{r} 41 \\ +\ 51 \\ \hline \end{array}$

11) $\begin{array}{r} 42 \\ +\ 53 \\ \hline \end{array}$
12) $\begin{array}{r} 70 \\ +\ 19 \\ \hline \end{array}$
13) $\begin{array}{r} 37 \\ +\ 11 \\ \hline \end{array}$
14) $\begin{array}{r} 78 \\ +\ 20 \\ \hline \end{array}$
15) $\begin{array}{r} 57 \\ +\ 32 \\ \hline \end{array}$

16) $\begin{array}{r} 81 \\ +\ 13 \\ \hline \end{array}$
17) $\begin{array}{r} 66 \\ +\ 23 \\ \hline \end{array}$
18) $\begin{array}{r} 71 \\ +\ 15 \\ \hline \end{array}$
19) $\begin{array}{r} 61 \\ +\ 27 \\ \hline \end{array}$
20) $\begin{array}{r} 15 \\ +\ 60 \\ \hline \end{array}$

21) $\begin{array}{r} 46 \\ +\ 13 \\ \hline \end{array}$
22) $\begin{array}{r} 88 \\ +\ 10 \\ \hline \end{array}$
23) $\begin{array}{r} 25 \\ +\ 34 \\ \hline \end{array}$
24) $\begin{array}{r} 74 \\ +\ 14 \\ \hline \end{array}$
25) $\begin{array}{r} 14 \\ +\ 10 \\ \hline \end{array}$

Double Digit Adding - No Regrouping

Date _____

1)
```
   41
+  51
_____
```

2)
```
   49
+  40
_____
```

3)
```
   15
+  14
_____
```

4)
```
   44
+  33
_____
```

5)
```
   62
+  24
_____
```

6)
```
   77
+  11
_____
```

7)
```
   86
+  11
_____
```

8)
```
   76
+  11
_____
```

9)
```
   18
+  21
_____
```

10)
```
   65
+  13
_____
```

11)
```
   72
+  22
_____
```

12)
```
   79
+  20
_____
```

13)
```
   10
+  29
_____
```

14)
```
   33
+  66
_____
```

15)
```
   53
+  20
_____
```

16)
```
   74
+  12
_____
```

17)
```
   25
+  51
_____
```

18)
```
   77
+  10
_____
```

19)
```
   36
+  21
_____
```

20)
```
   17
+  32
_____
```

21)
```
   52
+  47
_____
```

22)
```
   78
+  20
_____
```

23)
```
   88
+  10
_____
```

24)
```
   78
+  10
_____
```

25)
```
   73
+  20
_____
```

Name _____

Double Digit Adding - No Regrouping

Date _____

1) 26
  + 32

2) 71
  + 18

3) 33
  + 43

4) 48
  + 10

5) 68
  + 30

6) 88
  + 11

7) 56
  + 33

8) 38
  + 20

9) 18
  + 11

10) 57
   + 20

11) 22
   + 76

12) 31
   + 64

13) 19
   + 60

14) 62
   + 32

15) 77
   + 12

16) 88
   + 10

17) 11
   + 66

18) 75
   + 14

19) 28
   + 71

20) 19
   + 40

21) 23
   + 46

22) 77
   + 22

23) 73
   + 26

24) 28
   + 40

25) 83
   + 13

Name _____

Score /25

Double Digit Adding - No Regrouping

Date _____

1) 35
  + 11

2) 20
  + 77

3) 15
  + 60

4) 25
  + 61

5) 21
  + 73

6) 60
  + 25

7) 65
  + 14

8) 46
  + 50

9) 19
  + 30

10) 53
  + 44

11) 44
  + 25

12) 63
  + 12

13) 80
  + 13

14) 70
  + 10

15) 44
  + 30

16) 37
  + 21

17) 56
  + 20

18) 23
  + 25

19) 44
  + 41

20) 11
  + 34

21) 81
  + 10

22) 49
  + 10

23) 10
  + 19

24) 20
  + 49

25) 22
  + 37

DAY 10

Name _____

Date _____

Score __/25

1)   22
   + 33

2)   45
   + 20

3)   48
   + 41

4)   48
   + 21

5)   75
   + 23

6)   69
   + 20

7)   37
   + 31

8)   55
   + 32

9)   24
   + 71

10)   55
    + 34

11)   47
    + 20

12)   19
    + 20

13)   58
    + 10

14)   80
    + 12

15)   83
    + 13

16)   82
    + 10

17)   28
    + 10

18)   86
    + 10

19)   30
    + 20

20)   23
    + 34

21)   83
    + 14

22)   73
    + 22

23)   59
    + 10

24)   44
    + 50

25)   69
    + 20

Name _____

Double Digit Adding -Some Regrouping

Date _____

1) 47
  + 28

2) 33
  + 44

3) 27
  + 43

4) 17
  + 19

5) 15
  + 69

6) 70
  + 39

7) 30
  + 28

8) 98
  + 48

9) 60
  + 43

10) 30
  + 73

11) 21
  + 46

12) 38
  + 42

13) 87
  + 86

14) 60
  + 12

15) 20
  + 17

16) 87
  + 12

17) 77
  + 60

18) 43
  + 85

19) 83
  + 19

20) 61
  + 94

21) 82
  + 61

22) 78
  + 53

23) 97
  + 59

24) 85
  + 78

25) 72
  + 20

Name _____

Double Digit Adding -Some Regrouping   Date _____

1)   55
  + 89

2)   57
  + 64

3)   97
  + 32

4)   12
  + 73

5)   47
  + 21

6)   16
  + 85

7)   48
  + 90

8)   16
  + 44

9)   78
  + 94

10)   41
  + 27

11)   95
  + 29

12)   22
  + 64

13)   29
  + 82

14)   55
  + 41

15)   88
  + 13

16)   24
  + 54

17)   65
  + 75

18)   90
  + 39

19)   47
  + 84

20)   79
  + 30

21)   61
  + 40

22)   26
  + 18

23)   60
  + 51

24)   97
  + 45

25)   76
  + 58

DAY 13

Name _____

Double Digit Adding -Some Regrouping Date _____

1) 98 + 19	2) 56 + 33	3) 84 + 69	4) 31 + 63	5) 62 + 82
6) 14 + 10	7) 41 + 73	8) 11 + 22	9) 66 + 21	10) 43 + 38
11) 92 + 22	12) 62 + 39	13) 70 + 14	14) 23 + 94	15) 64 + 46
16) 37 + 71	17) 95 + 31	18) 18 + 69	19) 27 + 94	20) 53 + 65
21) 42 + 76	22) 91 + 21	23) 81 + 37	24) 24 + 42	25) 60 + 17

DAY 14

Name _____

Score /25

Double Digit Adding -Some Regrouping

Date _____

1) 80
  + 32

2) 88
  + 11

3) 83
  + 73

4) 60
  + 26

5) 93
  + 19

6) 89
  + 77

7) 88
  + 66

8) 43
  + 17

9) 89
  + 56

10) 74
   + 77

11) 17
   + 55

12) 39
   + 62

13) 96
   + 67

14) 20
   + 21

15) 86
   + 60

16) 15
   + 61

17) 80
   + 41

18) 61
   + 95

19) 69
   + 79

20) 42
   + 67

21) 10
   + 28

22) 21
   + 89

23) 10
   + 11

24) 81
   + 49

25) 33
   + 75

Name _____

Double Digit Adding -Some Regrouping

Date _____

1)   46
  + 49

2)   51
  + 62

3)   81
  + 57

4)   81
  + 17

5)   45
  + 22

6)   33
  + 77

7)   47
  + 73

8)   34
  + 45

9)   76
  + 74

10)   91
  + 29

11)   33
  + 39

12)   63
  + 66

13)   40
  + 56

14)   82
  + 77

15)   15
  + 32

16)   16
  + 10

17)   42
  + 88

18)   49
  + 50

19)   32
  + 42

20)   10
  + 64

21)   42
  + 92

22)   71
  + 12

23)   46
  + 19

24)   35
  + 29

25)   42
  + 58

DAY 16

Name _____

Score /25

Double Digit Adding -Some Regrouping Date _____

1)   44
+ 60

2)   85
+ 65

3)   79
+ 24

4)   10
+ 18

5)   71
+ 60

6)   86
+ 81

7)   42
+ 72

8)   36
+ 32

9)   61
+ 40

10)   36
+ 63

11)   74
+ 69

12)   43
+ 49

13)   92
+ 58

14)   20
+ 28

15)   24
+ 40

16)   18
+ 80

17)   16
+ 52

18)   28
+ 99

19)   52
+ 98

20)   56
+ 37

21)   47
+ 12

22)   18
+ 93

23)   19
+ 40

24)   48
+ 14

25)   71
+ 48

Name _____

Score /25

Date _____

1)   20
   + 69

2)   23
   + 74

3)   81
   + 18

4)   63
   + 72

5)   39
   + 53

6)   29
   + 41

7)   75
   + 47

8)   46
   + 82

9)   61
   + 33

10)   98
   + 88

11)   55
   + 91

12)   13
   + 44

13)   96
   + 26

14)   11
   + 15

15)   51
   + 24

16)   88
   + 57

17)   18
   + 82

18)   33
   + 91

19)   94
   + 20

20)   40
   + 79

21)   62
   + 74

22)   94
   + 46

23)   11
   + 10

24)   68
   + 45

25)   18
   + 65

Name _____

Double Digit Adding -Some Regrouping

Date _____

1) 22
  + 48
  _____

2) 38
  + 86
  _____

3) 10
  + 64
  _____

4) 52
  + 97
  _____

5) 15
  + 74
  _____

6) 81
  + 80
  _____

7) 10
  + 13
  _____

8) 83
  + 21
  _____

9) 48
  + 50
  _____

10) 69
  + 15
  _____

11) 66
  + 74
  _____

12) 79
  + 11
  _____

13) 74
  + 21
  _____

14) 64
  + 20
  _____

15) 66
  + 28
  _____

16) 74
  + 42
  _____

17) 51
  + 10
  _____

18) 81
  + 78
  _____

19) 98
  + 58
  _____

20) 99
  + 57
  _____

21) 52
  + 22
  _____

22) 25
  + 27
  _____

23) 17
  + 61
  _____

24) 37
  + 45
  _____

25) 69
  + 58
  _____

DAY 19

Name _____

Score /25

Double Digit Adding -Some Regrouping Date _____

1) 67
  + 38

2) 36
  + 62

3) 40
  + 21

4) 36
  + 10

5) 72
  + 34

6) 77
  + 49

7) 54
  + 64

8) 32
  + 93

9) 45
  + 43

10) 72
  + 62

11) 38
  + 19

12) 28
  + 78

13) 23
  + 58

14) 85
  + 41

15) 58
  + 74

16) 96
  + 56

17) 91
  + 24

18) 18
  + 92

19) 80
  + 36

20) 78
  + 66

21) 61
  + 89

22) 77
  + 50

23) 21
  + 35

24) 26
  + 52

25) 57
  + 53

19

DAY 20

Score /25

Double Digit Adding -Some Regrouping

Date _____

1) 53
  + 94
  ‾‾‾‾

2) 55
  + 80
  ‾‾‾‾

3) 63
  + 68
  ‾‾‾‾

4) 64
  + 85
  ‾‾‾‾

5) 42
  + 71
  ‾‾‾‾

6) 64
  + 78
  ‾‾‾‾

7) 78
  + 64
  ‾‾‾‾

8) 70
  + 87
  ‾‾‾‾

9) 65
  + 59
  ‾‾‾‾

10) 23
  + 55
  ‾‾‾‾

11) 15
  + 87
  ‾‾‾‾

12) 41
  + 51
  ‾‾‾‾

13) 22
  + 14
  ‾‾‾‾

14) 31
  + 88
  ‾‾‾‾

15) 69
  + 77
  ‾‾‾‾

16) 66
  + 40
  ‾‾‾‾

17) 57
  + 71
  ‾‾‾‾

18) 84
  + 87
  ‾‾‾‾

19) 72
  + 13
  ‾‾‾‾

20) 42
  + 53
  ‾‾‾‾

21) 15
  + 39
  ‾‾‾‾

22) 92
  + 38
  ‾‾‾‾

23) 18
  + 29
  ‾‾‾‾

24) 25
  + 31
  ‾‾‾‾

25) 67
  + 45
  ‾‾‾‾

Name _____

Triple Digit Adding - No Regrouping   Date _____

1) 454
  + 513

2) 495
  + 402

3) 710
  + 149

4) 565
  + 411

5) 283
  + 605

6) 393
  + 602

7) 677
  + 110

8) 636
  + 252

9) 267
  + 621

10) 207
  + 751

11) 595
  + 300

12) 806
  + 173

13) 804
  + 181

14) 413
  + 214

15) 533
  + 311

16) 279
  + 600

17) 151
  + 413

18) 775
  + 220

19) 622
  + 110

20) 427
  + 330

21) 852
  + 104

22) 468
  + 100

23) 718
  + 150

24) 169
  + 410

25) 258
  + 321

DAY 22

Name _____

Triple Digit Adding - No Regrouping

Date _____

1) 391
  + 108

2) 325
  + 110

3) 360
  + 123

4) 300
  + 162

5) 184
  + 403

6) 189
  + 810

7) 441
  + 232

8) 565
  + 200

9) 656
  + 101

10) 321
   + 403

11) 213
   + 426

12) 362
   + 336

13) 304
   + 363

14) 340
   + 614

15) 573
   + 101

16) 424
   + 363

17) 238
   + 520

18) 242
   + 627

19) 356
   + 621

20) 274
   + 514

21) 360
   + 301

22) 764
   + 203

23) 774
   + 122

24) 819
   + 170

25) 763
   + 112

DAY 23

Score /25

Triple Digit Adding - No Regrouping

Date _____

1) 310
  + 127

2) 228
  + 351

3) 443
  + 240

4) 352
  + 531

5) 488
  + 300

6) 573
  + 311

7) 480
  + 407

8) 314
  + 354

9) 856
  + 113

10) 368
   + 121

11) 497
   + 501

12) 810
   + 143

13) 119
   + 300

14) 676
   + 111

15) 334
   + 120

16) 894
   + 104

17) 255
   + 741

18) 546
   + 102

19) 464
   + 102

20) 355
   + 441

21) 160
   + 734

22) 460
   + 420

23) 610
   + 323

24) 432
   + 235

25) 877
   + 111

DAY 24

Name _____

Triple Digit Adding - No Regrouping

Date _____

1) 278
  + 111

2) 662
  + 124

3) 691
  + 100

4) 645
  + 220

5) 705
  + 121

6) 231
  + 214

7) 574
  + 401

8) 341
  + 211

9) 860
  + 102

10) 237
   + 152

11) 713
   + 124

12) 740
   + 219

13) 710
   + 205

14) 450
   + 206

15) 191
   + 506

16) 108
   + 551

17) 775
   + 122

18) 350
   + 239

19) 372
   + 222

20) 102
   + 217

21) 678
   + 200

22) 834
   + 161

23) 629
   + 300

24) 313
   + 352

25) 730
   + 222

Name _____

Score /25

Triple Digit Adding - No Regrouping   Date _____

1) 393
  + 105

2) 550
  + 301

3) 186
  + 603

4) 526
  + 172

5) 213
  + 372

6) 377
  + 410

7) 138
  + 541

8) 787
  + 100

9) 185
  + 400

10) 551
   + 303

11) 322
   + 304

12) 819
   + 180

13) 837
   + 102

14) 115
   + 561

15) 354
   + 111

16) 381
   + 517

17) 563
   + 335

18) 435
   + 564

19) 277
   + 120

20) 742
   + 254

21) 319
   + 670

22) 188
   + 211

23) 770
   + 225

24) 497
   + 402

25) 719
   + 210

Name _____

Triple Digit Adding - No Regrouping

Date _____

1) 737 + 101

2) 638 + 141

3) 416 + 521

4) 648 + 330

5) 714 + 173

6) 722 + 120

7) 191 + 505

8) 560 + 332

9) 621 + 238

10) 306 + 673

11) 812 + 183

12) 648 + 310

13) 248 + 710

14) 150 + 335

15) 611 + 326

16) 425 + 540

17) 199 + 200

18) 860 + 112

19) 738 + 200

20) 523 + 105

21) 331 + 435

22) 164 + 635

23) 886 + 103

24) 406 + 543

25) 681 + 305

Name _____

Triple Digit Adding - No Regrouping

Date _____

1) 227
  + 170

2) 543
  + 214

3) 769
  + 210

4) 116
  + 222

5) 671
  + 303

6) 219
  + 410

7) 526
  + 203

8) 699
  + 100

9) 845
  + 101

10) 506
  + 111

11) 564
  + 404

12) 407
  + 251

13) 522
  + 271

14) 681
  + 306

15) 564
  + 302

16) 687
  + 310

17) 185
  + 610

18) 379
  + 100

19) 515
  + 254

20) 541
  + 342

21) 524
  + 222

22) 177
  + 300

23) 507
  + 372

24) 898
  + 101

25) 221
  + 111

Name _____

Triple Digit Adding - No Regrouping   Date _____

1) 698
  + 300

2) 328
  + 671

3) 569
  + 100

4) 206
  + 191

5) 377
  + 321

6) 344
  + 435

7) 256
  + 532

8) 222
  + 227

9) 684
  + 205

10) 895
   + 104

11) 295
   + 103

12) 148
   + 121

13) 648
   + 300

14) 423
   + 156

15) 711
   + 224

16) 291
   + 200

17) 227
   + 311

18) 819
   + 130

19) 696
   + 100

20) 746
   + 101

21) 189
   + 710

22) 250
   + 744

23) 872
   + 103

24) 811
   + 123

25) 304
   + 171

Name _____

Triple Digit Adding - No Regrouping   Date _____

1) 437
  + 332

2) 845
  + 131

3) 609
  + 220

4) 225
  + 362

5) 458
  + 300

6) 713
  + 135

7) 701
  + 200

8) 136
  + 761

9) 470
  + 208

10) 338
   + 610

11) 802
   + 174

12) 832
   + 107

13) 120
   + 158

14) 222
   + 417

15) 187
   + 311

16) 128
   + 551

17) 355
   + 501

18) 135
   + 114

19) 389
   + 200

20) 451
   + 303

21) 105
   + 471

22) 229
   + 760

23) 774
   + 120

24) 751
   + 218

25) 718
   + 101

Name _____

Triple Digit Adding - No Regrouping

Date _____

1)
$$
\begin{array}{r}
896 \\
+\ 101 \\
\hline
\end{array}
$$

2)
$$
\begin{array}{r}
405 \\
+\ 173 \\
\hline
\end{array}
$$

3)
$$
\begin{array}{r}
849 \\
+\ 100 \\
\hline
\end{array}
$$

4)
$$
\begin{array}{r}
379 \\
+\ 600 \\
\hline
\end{array}
$$

5)
$$
\begin{array}{r}
798 \\
+\ 100 \\
\hline
\end{array}
$$

6)
$$
\begin{array}{r}
267 \\
+\ 310 \\
\hline
\end{array}
$$

7)
$$
\begin{array}{r}
404 \\
+\ 394 \\
\hline
\end{array}
$$

8)
$$
\begin{array}{r}
655 \\
+\ 313 \\
\hline
\end{array}
$$

9)
$$
\begin{array}{r}
373 \\
+\ 424 \\
\hline
\end{array}
$$

10)
$$
\begin{array}{r}
251 \\
+\ 428 \\
\hline
\end{array}
$$

11)
$$
\begin{array}{r}
692 \\
+\ 202 \\
\hline
\end{array}
$$

12)
$$
\begin{array}{r}
509 \\
+\ 380 \\
\hline
\end{array}
$$

13)
$$
\begin{array}{r}
502 \\
+\ 141 \\
\hline
\end{array}
$$

14)
$$
\begin{array}{r}
465 \\
+\ 524 \\
\hline
\end{array}
$$

15)
$$
\begin{array}{r}
376 \\
+\ 123 \\
\hline
\end{array}
$$

16)
$$
\begin{array}{r}
658 \\
+\ 130 \\
\hline
\end{array}
$$

17)
$$
\begin{array}{r}
613 \\
+\ 144 \\
\hline
\end{array}
$$

18)
$$
\begin{array}{r}
623 \\
+\ 101 \\
\hline
\end{array}
$$

19)
$$
\begin{array}{r}
258 \\
+\ 410 \\
\hline
\end{array}
$$

20)
$$
\begin{array}{r}
263 \\
+\ 515 \\
\hline
\end{array}
$$

21)
$$
\begin{array}{r}
103 \\
+\ 714 \\
\hline
\end{array}
$$

22)
$$
\begin{array}{r}
455 \\
+\ 342 \\
\hline
\end{array}
$$

23)
$$
\begin{array}{r}
210 \\
+\ 131 \\
\hline
\end{array}
$$

24)
$$
\begin{array}{r}
828 \\
+\ 140 \\
\hline
\end{array}
$$

25)
$$
\begin{array}{r}
718 \\
+\ 101 \\
\hline
\end{array}
$$

Name _____

Triple Digit Adding - Some Regrouping   Date _____

1)   176
   + 167

2)   693
   + 983

3)   417
   + 332

4)   861
   + 849

5)   396
   + 316

6)   658
   + 541

7)   646
   + 681

8)   616
   + 699

9)   957
   + 251

10)   423
    + 188

11)   539
    + 718

12)   874
    + 391

13)   776
    + 100

14)   350
    + 724

15)   264
    + 958

16)   664
    + 632

17)   790
    + 918

18)   420
    + 866

19)   128
    + 637

20)   826
    + 876

21)   154
    + 313

22)   583
    + 540

23)   223
    + 312

24)   821
    + 430

25)   590
    + 118

DAY 32

Name _____

Date _____

Score /25

1) 689
  + 563

2) 492
  + 516

3) 206
  + 265

4) 127
  + 643

5) 861
  + 349

6) 323
  + 105

7) 248
  + 481

8) 413
  + 628

9) 605
  + 228

10) 203
  + 388

11) 966
  + 576

12) 310
  + 296

13) 467
  + 861

14) 756
  + 722

15) 284
  + 935

16) 889
  + 872

17) 344
  + 891

18) 870
  + 590

19) 936
  + 805

20) 220
  + 840

21) 251
  + 509

22) 372
  + 725

23) 362
  + 772

24) 945
  + 212

25) 781
  + 695

Name _____

Triple Digit Adding - Some Regrouping

Date _____

1) 792
  + 486

2) 854
  + 130

3) 460
  + 861

4) 750
  + 330

5) 798
  + 738

6) 773
  + 835

7) 438
  + 372

8) 394
  + 802

9) 396
  + 275

10) 409
   + 893

11) 393
   + 240

12) 755
   + 811

13) 753
   + 439

14) 206
   + 347

15) 135
   + 745

16) 371
   + 618

17) 585
   + 835

18) 188
   + 882

19) 974
   + 481

20) 210
   + 667

21) 439
   + 321

22) 597
   + 546

23) 547
   + 344

24) 991
   + 274

25) 945
   + 754

Name _____

Score /25

Triple Digit Adding - Some Regrouping

Date _____

1) 468
  + 872

2) 374
  + 349

3) 761
  + 357

4) 858
  + 262

5) 683
  + 152

6) 793
  + 440

7) 699
  + 381

8) 398
  + 703

9) 611
  + 668

10) 160
   + 931

11) 156
   + 251

12) 272
   + 185

13) 702
   + 870

14) 904
   + 327

15) 907
   + 599

16) 129
   + 142

17) 345
   + 577

18) 955
   + 823

19) 685
   + 268

20) 102
   + 517

21) 947
   + 694

22) 551
   + 127

23) 610
   + 936

24) 808
   + 481

25) 231
   + 323

Name _____

Triple Digit Adding - Some Regrouping   Date _____

1) 763
  + 790

2) 101
  + 269

3) 733
  + 924

4) 264
  + 260

5) 108
  + 388

6) 360
  + 578

7) 296
  + 632

8) 674
  + 966

9) 708
  + 617

10) 370
   + 572

11) 293
   + 910

12) 939
   + 483

13) 143
   + 754

14) 617
   + 291

15) 703
   + 699

16) 236
   + 370

17) 240
   + 151

18) 232
   + 693

19) 423
   + 291

20) 958
   + 485

21) 217
   + 323

22) 598
   + 624

23) 972
   + 896

24) 619
   + 288

25) 271
   + 912

DAY 36

Name _____

Score /25

Date _____

1)   987
+   944

2)   179
+   649

3)   865
+   843

4)   606
+   444

5)   875
+   489

6)   443
+   347

7)   715
+   756

8)   979
+   271

9)   862
+   828

10)   747
+   666

11)   695
+   841

12)   319
+   438

13)   616
+   348

14)   937
+   900

15)   476
+   741

16)   247
+   802

17)   522
+   826

18)   901
+   248

19)   479
+   777

20)   994
+   362

21)   777
+   497

22)   708
+   370

23)   824
+   269

24)   208
+   245

25)   183
+   417

Name _____

Triple Digit Adding - Some Regrouping   Date _____

1)   368
   + 676

2)   705
   + 551

3)   598
   + 854

4)   398
   + 888

5)   921
   + 194

6)   918
   + 722

7)   368
   + 521

8)   364
   + 930

9)   575
   + 998

10)   937
   + 535

11)   158
   + 753

12)   206
   + 746

13)   427
   + 318

14)   869
   + 386

15)   435
   + 412

16)   175
   + 367

17)   169
   + 476

18)   463
   + 816

19)   822
   + 492

20)   794
   + 942

21)   263
   + 445

22)   622
   + 709

23)   913
   + 890

24)   936
   + 399

25)   560
   + 902

DAY 38

Name _____

Triple Digit Adding - Some Regrouping

Date _____

1)   122
 + 568

2)   908
 + 346

3)   643
 + 307

4)   874
 + 357

5)   930
 + 682

6)   294
 + 948

7)   966
 + 207

8)   675
 + 719

9)   873
 + 946

10)   217
 + 819

11)   539
 + 413

12)   672
 + 929

13)   126
 + 673

14)   793
 + 529

15)   838
 + 245

16)   102
 + 283

17)   564
 + 772

18)   430
 + 446

19)   343
 + 894

20)   950
 + 655

21)   455
 + 770

22)   276
 + 518

23)   480
 + 156

24)   518
 + 855

25)   884
 + 538

Name _____

Triple Digit Adding - Some Regrouping

Date _____

1)   860
   + 443

2)   272
   + 142

3)   503
   + 607

4)   979
   + 180

5)   736
   + 625

6)   129
   + 909

7)   441
   + 101

8)   840
   + 287

9)   262
   + 756

10)   601
    + 232

11)   959
    + 967

12)   744
    + 509

13)   146
    + 159

14)   734
    + 127

15)   118
    + 600

16)   736
    + 895

17)   578
    + 909

18)   757
    + 684

19)   114
    + 124

20)   519
    + 138

21)   732
    + 226

22)   299
    + 721

23)   142
    + 662

24)   648
    + 673

25)   753
    + 338

Name _____

Triple Digit Adding - Some Regrouping

Date _____

1)   602
  + 234

2)   627
  + 581

3)   914
  + 164

4)   691
  + 663

5)   964
  + 519

6)   952
  + 924

7)   457
  + 464

8)   774
  + 977

9)   823
  + 771

10)   913
  + 885

11)   884
  + 857

12)   831
  + 298

13)   877
  + 692

14)   855
  + 951

15)   747
  + 449

16)   674
  + 499

17)   391
  + 552

18)   394
  + 776

19)   907
  + 501

20)   952
  + 523

21)   208
  + 507

22)   637
  + 101

23)   641
  + 982

24)   791
  + 546

25)   795
  + 139

DAY 41

Name _____

Date _____

Score /25

1) 34 - 30	2) 56 - 45	3) 78 - 67	4) 51 - 41	5) 63 - 21
6) 86 - 44	7) 23 - 12	8) 36 - 32	9) 17 - 10	10) 91 - 11
11) 96 - 93	12) 93 - 10	13) 21 - 10	14) 82 - 71	15) 29 - 19
16) 83 - 70	17) 38 - 11	18) 41 - 20	19) 91 - 10	20) 54 - 40
21) 88 - 60	22) 48 - 43	23) 82 - 31	24) 36 - 14	25) 15 - 10

DAY 42

Name _____

Double Digit Subtraction - No Regrouping   Date _____

1)
$$\begin{array}{r} 75 \\ -\ 31 \\ \hline \end{array}$$

2)
$$\begin{array}{r} 42 \\ -\ 31 \\ \hline \end{array}$$

3)
$$\begin{array}{r} 56 \\ -\ 21 \\ \hline \end{array}$$

4)
$$\begin{array}{r} 92 \\ -\ 42 \\ \hline \end{array}$$

5)
$$\begin{array}{r} 75 \\ -\ 52 \\ \hline \end{array}$$

6)
$$\begin{array}{r} 77 \\ -\ 63 \\ \hline \end{array}$$

7)
$$\begin{array}{r} 35 \\ -\ 21 \\ \hline \end{array}$$

8)
$$\begin{array}{r} 45 \\ -\ 30 \\ \hline \end{array}$$

9)
$$\begin{array}{r} 22 \\ -\ 12 \\ \hline \end{array}$$

10)
$$\begin{array}{r} 46 \\ -\ 31 \\ \hline \end{array}$$

11)
$$\begin{array}{r} 97 \\ -\ 62 \\ \hline \end{array}$$

12)
$$\begin{array}{r} 72 \\ -\ 61 \\ \hline \end{array}$$

13)
$$\begin{array}{r} 67 \\ -\ 37 \\ \hline \end{array}$$

14)
$$\begin{array}{r} 73 \\ -\ 33 \\ \hline \end{array}$$

15)
$$\begin{array}{r} 41 \\ -\ 10 \\ \hline \end{array}$$

16)
$$\begin{array}{r} 42 \\ -\ 21 \\ \hline \end{array}$$

17)
$$\begin{array}{r} 75 \\ -\ 13 \\ \hline \end{array}$$

18)
$$\begin{array}{r} 99 \\ -\ 23 \\ \hline \end{array}$$

19)
$$\begin{array}{r} 93 \\ -\ 12 \\ \hline \end{array}$$

20)
$$\begin{array}{r} 71 \\ -\ 41 \\ \hline \end{array}$$

21)
$$\begin{array}{r} 76 \\ -\ 11 \\ \hline \end{array}$$

22)
$$\begin{array}{r} 82 \\ -\ 62 \\ \hline \end{array}$$

23)
$$\begin{array}{r} 77 \\ -\ 12 \\ \hline \end{array}$$

24)
$$\begin{array}{r} 88 \\ -\ 72 \\ \hline \end{array}$$

25)
$$\begin{array}{r} 68 \\ -\ 11 \\ \hline \end{array}$$

Name _____

Double Digit Subtraction - No Regrouping   Date _____

1)   73
   - 60

2)   11
   - 10

3)   64
   - 14

4)   43
   - 31

5)   56
   - 15

6)   85
   - 42

7)   51
   - 10

8)   21
   - 10

9)   89
   - 81

10)   47
   - 30

11)   58
   - 14

12)   91
   - 21

13)   85
   - 65

14)   38
   - 28

15)   76
   - 15

16)   54
   - 10

17)   76
   - 54

18)   89
   - 38

19)   71
   - 51

20)   21
   - 11

21)   92
   - 30

22)   68
   - 48

23)   24
   - 22

24)   43
   - 22

25)   31
   - 11

Name _____

Double Digit Subtraction - No Regrouping Date _____

1) 49
  - 32

2) 96
  - 31

3) 26
  - 23

4) 95
  - 85

5) 83
  - 33

6) 68
  - 15

7) 77
  - 74

8) 94
  - 32

9) 38
  - 22

10) 86
   - 61

11) 64
   - 10

12) 18
   - 15

13) 41
   - 20

14) 29
   - 16

15) 57
   - 10

16) 91
   - 30

17) 43
   - 13

18) 74
   - 72

19) 69
   - 65

20) 93
   - 62

21) 72
   - 60

22) 98
   - 22

23) 75
   - 63

24) 95
   - 72

25) 43
   - 22

Name _____

Double Digit Subtraction - No Regrouping   Date _____

1)   57
-   16

2)   44
-   20

3)   75
-   15

4)   65
-   20

5)   23
-   21

6)   46
-   15

7)   34
-   31

8)   73
-   23

9)   64
-   41

10)   58
-   17

11)   14
-   11

12)   28
-   20

13)   98
-   70

14)   21
-   11

15)   72
-   31

16)   72
-   60

17)   53
-   51

18)   36
-   21

19)   34
-   32

20)   62
-   52

21)   92
-   71

22)   52
-   21

23)   82
-   31

24)   96
-   73

25)   66
-   45

Name _____

Double Digit Subtraction - No Regrouping   Date _____

1) 95
  - 95
  ____

2) 18
  - 12
  ____

3) 72
  - 31
  ____

4) 53
  - 21
  ____

5) 62
  - 12
  ____

6) 67
  - 15
  ____

7) 78
  - 35
  ____

8) 25
  - 15
  ____

9) 75
  - 61
  ____

10) 77
  - 24
  ____

11) 34
  - 32
  ____

12) 95
  - 53
  ____

13) 57
  - 23
  ____

14) 75
  - 50
  ____

15) 97
  - 15
  ____

16) 97
  - 76
  ____

17) 45
  - 23
  ____

18) 74
  - 43
  ____

19) 14
  - 11
  ____

20) 88
  - 77
  ____

21) 28
  - 20
  ____

22) 64
  - 12
  ____

23) 98
  - 15
  ____

24) 38
  - 18
  ____

25) 75
  - 52
  ____

DAY 47

Double Digit Subtraction - No Regrouping

Date _____

1) 67
 - 50

2) 57
 - 26

3) 57
 - 50

4) 81
 - 40

5) 41
 - 20

6) 37
 - 20

7) 48
 - 30

8) 84
 - 52

9) 79
 - 36

10) 52
 - 30

11) 71
 - 21

12) 96
 - 82

13) 34
 - 24

14) 38
 - 12

15) 72
 - 52

16) 72
 - 60

17) 21
 - 10

18) 96
 - 83

19) 26
 - 14

20) 86
 - 44

21) 23
 - 21

22) 89
 - 22

23) 72
 - 32

24) 66
 - 21

25) 25
 - 12

Name _____

Double Digit Subtraction - No Regrouping   Date _____

1) 86
   - 25
   _____

2) 93
   - 51
   _____

3) 67
   - 30
   _____

4) 52
   - 12
   _____

5) 57
   - 12
   _____

6) 54
   - 42
   _____

7) 99
   - 49
   _____

8) 89
   - 62
   _____

9) 74
   - 34
   _____

10) 86
    - 60
    _____

11) 92
    - 10
    _____

12) 77
    - 26
    _____

13) 33
    - 23
    _____

14) 95
    - 33
    _____

15) 63
    - 41
    _____

16) 43
    - 22
    _____

17) 21
    - 10
    _____

18) 39
    - 20
    _____

19) 81
    - 10
    _____

20) 78
    - 40
    _____

21) 53
    - 33
    _____

22) 84
    - 23
    _____

23) 67
    - 53
    _____

24) 91
    - 30
    _____

25) 32
    - 20
    _____

Name _____

Double Digit Subtraction - No Regrouping   Date _____

1)   71
   - 51
   _____

2)   39
   - 19
   _____

3)   72
   - 61
   _____

4)   83
   - 53
   _____

5)   98
   - 94
   _____

6)   53
   - 40
   _____

7)   38
   - 12
   _____

8)   84
   - 40
   _____

9)   81
   - 71
   _____

10)   71
   - 10
   _____

11)   86
   - 72
   _____

12)   55
   - 13
   _____

13)   71
   - 21
   _____

14)   84
   - 30
   _____

15)   34
   - 31
   _____

16)   18
   - 14
   _____

17)   97
   - 14
   _____

18)   83
   - 60
   _____

19)   82
   - 20
   _____

20)   32
   - 11
   _____

21)   35
   - 30
   _____

22)   69
   - 55
   _____

23)   71
   - 30
   _____

24)   83
   - 50
   _____

25)   38
   - 18
   _____

DAY 50

Name _____

Double Digit Subtraction - No Regrouping   Date _____

1) $\begin{array}{r} 34 \\ -\ 24 \\ \hline \end{array}$
2) $\begin{array}{r} 78 \\ -\ 22 \\ \hline \end{array}$
3) $\begin{array}{r} 12 \\ -\ 11 \\ \hline \end{array}$
4) $\begin{array}{r} 54 \\ -\ 31 \\ \hline \end{array}$
5) $\begin{array}{r} 61 \\ -\ 51 \\ \hline \end{array}$

6) $\begin{array}{r} 46 \\ -\ 30 \\ \hline \end{array}$
7) $\begin{array}{r} 15 \\ -\ 11 \\ \hline \end{array}$
8) $\begin{array}{r} 83 \\ -\ 10 \\ \hline \end{array}$
9) $\begin{array}{r} 71 \\ -\ 60 \\ \hline \end{array}$
10) $\begin{array}{r} 52 \\ -\ 40 \\ \hline \end{array}$

11) $\begin{array}{r} 18 \\ -\ 10 \\ \hline \end{array}$
12) $\begin{array}{r} 33 \\ -\ 30 \\ \hline \end{array}$
13) $\begin{array}{r} 55 \\ -\ 25 \\ \hline \end{array}$
14) $\begin{array}{r} 98 \\ -\ 47 \\ \hline \end{array}$
15) $\begin{array}{r} 95 \\ -\ 65 \\ \hline \end{array}$

16) $\begin{array}{r} 82 \\ -\ 42 \\ \hline \end{array}$
17) $\begin{array}{r} 49 \\ -\ 37 \\ \hline \end{array}$
18) $\begin{array}{r} 37 \\ -\ 13 \\ \hline \end{array}$
19) $\begin{array}{r} 97 \\ -\ 25 \\ \hline \end{array}$
20) $\begin{array}{r} 85 \\ -\ 24 \\ \hline \end{array}$

21) $\begin{array}{r} 16 \\ -\ 12 \\ \hline \end{array}$
22) $\begin{array}{r} 83 \\ -\ 71 \\ \hline \end{array}$
23) $\begin{array}{r} 55 \\ -\ 35 \\ \hline \end{array}$
24) $\begin{array}{r} 85 \\ -\ 44 \\ \hline \end{array}$
25) $\begin{array}{r} 53 \\ -\ 50 \\ \hline \end{array}$

Name _____

Double Digit Subtraction - Some Regrouping

Date _____

1) 73 - 14	2) 98 - 56	3) 77 - 19	4) 65 - 43	5) 69 - 45
6) 91 - 20	7) 85 - 43	8) 65 - 63	9) 97 - 38	10) 97 - 82
11) 68 - 45	12) 94 - 72	13) 89 - 40	14) 35 - 19	15) 57 - 48
16) 61 - 45	17) 93 - 90	18) 94 - 92	19) 84 - 46	20) 73 - 67
21) 86 - 80	22) 82 - 66	23) 87 - 49	24) 96 - 92	25) 97 - 91

DAY 52

Name _____

Double Digit Subtraction - Some Regrouping

Date _____

1) 65
  - 23

2) 75
  - 68

3) 80
  - 75

4) 95
  - 49

5) 99
  - 63

6) 68
  - 65

7) 40
  - 25

8) 92
  - 49

9) 72
  - 63

10) 74
   - 56

11) 95
   - 29

12) 59
   - 10

13) 80
   - 36

14) 93
   - 74

15) 97
   - 72

16) 61
   - 39

17) 95
   - 12

18) 75
   - 73

19) 95
   - 88

20) 74
   - 38

21) 89
   - 57

22) 78
   - 20

23) 70
   - 21

24) 35
   - 24

25) 94
   - 81

DAY 53

Name _____

Score /25

Double Digit Subtraction - Some Regrouping   Date _____

1)   98
   - 94

2)   44
   - 31

3)   86
   - 20

4)   35
   - 16

5)   88
   - 19

6)   99
   - 80

7)   63
   - 56

8)   74
   - 11

9)   86
   - 59

10)   86
    - 43

11)   77
    - 49

12)   99
    - 62

13)   98
    - 29

14)   92
    - 17

15)   75
    - 55

16)   64
    - 42

17)   98
    - 69

18)   54
    - 38

19)   94
    - 41

20)   88
    - 76

21)   88
    - 65

22)   87
    - 21

23)   98
    - 53

24)   68
    - 31

25)   88
    - 62

DAY 54

Name _____

Date _____

Score __/25

1) 94
  - 62

2) 89
  - 67

3) 95
  - 88

4) 84
  - 73

5) 91
  - 52

6) 80
  - 69

7) 75
  - 57

8) 87
  - 83

9) 62
  - 32

10) 63
   - 20

11) 59
   - 42

12) 99
   - 94

13) 70
   - 52

14) 60
   - 27

15) 96
   - 94

16) 90
   - 36

17) 99
   - 74

18) 75
   - 71

19) 72
   - 44

20) 96
   - 47

21) 22
   - 19

22) 57
   - 47

23) 72
   - 46

24) 70
   - 36

25) 72
   - 24

Name _____

Double Digit Subtraction - Some Regrouping Date _____

1)   64
   - 58

2)   90
   - 72

3)   91
   - 87

4)   62
   - 43

5)   56
   - 42

6)   98
   - 65

7)   79
   - 40

8)   82
   - 42

9)   85
   - 35

10)   71
   - 67

11)   51
   - 36

12)   55
   - 10

13)   48
   - 42

14)   74
   - 71

15)   70
   - 32

16)   86
   - 15

17)   58
   - 11

18)   80
   - 54

19)   75
   - 15

20)   85
   - 49

21)   94
   - 82

22)   97
   - 87

23)   97
   - 83

24)   90
   - 85

25)   91
   - 80

Name _____

Score
/25

Double Digit Subtraction - Some Regrouping   Date _____

1)   99
   - 83

2)   99
   - 90

3)   98
   - 42

4)   33
   - 29

5)   77
   - 64

6)   91
   - 85

7)   84
   - 52

8)   81
   - 43

9)   56
   - 34

10)   98
    - 24

11)   99
    - 88

12)   67
    - 63

13)   81
    - 23

14)   55
    - 40

15)   91
    - 15

16)   80
    - 62

17)   89
    - 31

18)   95
    - 15

19)   57
    - 43

20)   87
    - 14

21)   62
    - 56

22)   78
    - 41

23)   89
    - 17

24)   90
    - 18

25)   78
    - 50

Name _____

Double Digit Subtraction - Some Regrouping   Date _____

1) 73
  - 30

2) 95
  - 93

3) 86
  - 64

4) 94
  - 45

5) 35
  - 22

6) 90
  - 35

7) 69
  - 21

8) 42
  - 32

9) 71
  - 39

10) 64
   - 42

11) 82
   - 78

12) 68
   - 43

13) 90
   - 35

14) 95
   - 53

15) 88
   - 19

16) 65
   - 51

17) 74
   - 68

18) 91
   - 58

19) 72
   - 30

20) 80
   - 78

21) 21
   - 17

22) 57
   - 44

23) 94
   - 76

24) 97
   - 93

25) 86
   - 10

Name _____

Double Digit Subtraction - Some Regrouping   Date _____

1)   86
   - 77

2)   80
   - 31

3)   76
   - 68

4)   84
   - 81

5)   97
   - 84

6)   98
   - 34

7)   92
   - 19

8)   76
   - 71

9)   83
   - 43

10)   18
   - 14

11)   86
   - 72

12)   67
   - 32

13)   93
   - 85

14)   92
   - 66

15)   61
   - 57

16)   94
   - 57

17)   62
   - 44

18)   40
   - 14

19)   34
   - 22

20)   52
   - 20

21)   95
   - 80

22)   79
   - 73

23)   37
   - 16

24)   97
   - 80

25)   39
   - 23

Name _____

Score

/25

Double Digit Subtraction - Some Regrouping Date _____

1)   96
   - 92

2)   98
   - 37

3)   31
   - 27

4)   44
   - 27

5)   75
   - 50

6)   84
   - 12

7)   79
   - 73

8)   81
   - 35

9)   90
   - 75

10)   62
   - 60

11)   93
   - 76

12)   79
   - 55

13)   76
   - 54

14)   87
   - 54

15)   71
   - 57

16)   84
   - 71

17)   71
   - 33

18)   97
   - 75

19)   60
   - 40

20)   87
   - 30

21)   56
   - 45

22)   82
   - 70

23)   87
   - 79

24)   88
   - 44

25)   63
   - 19

DAY 60

Name _____

Double Digit Subtraction - Some Regrouping Date _____

1) $83 - 44$

2) $48 - 24$

3) $97 - 87$

4) $48 - 41$

5) $92 - 89$

6) $55 - 52$

7) $92 - 81$

8) $66 - 39$

9) $98 - 95$

10) $99 - 57$

11) $97 - 71$

12) $69 - 62$

13) $64 - 62$

14) $99 - 74$

15) $80 - 19$

16) $41 - 12$

17) $96 - 71$

18) $50 - 40$

19) $67 - 56$

20) $85 - 47$

21) $89 - 73$

22) $93 - 38$

23) $62 - 57$

24) $91 - 70$

25) $96 - 69$

Name _____

Score /25

Triple Digit Subtraction - No Regrouping

Date _____

1) 458
  - 425

2) 211
  - 201

3) 929
  - 400

4) 915
  - 101

5) 597
  - 403

6) 599
  - 433

7) 821
  - 310

8) 251
  - 220

9) 758
  - 643

10) 742
  - 520

11) 796
  - 745

12) 185
  - 161

13) 658
  - 610

14) 791
  - 630

15) 499
  - 395

16) 285
  - 274

17) 688
  - 387

18) 565
  - 432

19) 749
  - 131

20) 345
  - 321

21) 662
  - 122

22) 884
  - 403

23) 616
  - 405

24) 889
  - 706

25) 832
  - 312

DAY 62

Name _____

Triple Digit Subtraction - No Regrouping

Date _____

1) 465
  - 213

2) 532
  - 422

3) 742
  - 512

4) 898
  - 758

5) 466
  - 312

6) 769
  - 204

7) 772
  - 502

8) 637
  - 430

9) 526
  - 116

10) 689
   - 562

11) 299
   - 201

12) 371
   - 161

13) 448
   - 113

14) 647
   - 141

15) 992
   - 962

16) 695
   - 495

17) 432
   - 411

18) 238
   - 137

19) 414
   - 214

20) 777
   - 132

21) 198
   - 138

22) 528
   - 100

23) 119
   - 102

24) 518
   - 404

25) 567
   - 323

Triple Digit Subtraction - No Regrouping

Date _____

1) 996
  - 583

2) 735
  - 733

3) 397
  - 144

4) 786
  - 310

5) 725
  - 611

6) 327
  - 214

7) 337
  - 322

8) 911
  - 801

9) 612
  - 110

10) 718
  - 305

11) 373
  - 261

12) 857
  - 354

13) 358
  - 337

14) 565
  - 454

15) 882
  - 140

16) 685
  - 285

17) 251
  - 100

18) 688
  - 575

19) 821
  - 411

20) 764
  - 633

21) 221
  - 101

22) 772
  - 340

23) 762
  - 610

24) 535
  - 520

25) 282
  - 121

Triple Digit Subtraction - No Regrouping   Date _____

1) 923
  - 502

2) 847
  - 615

3) 352
  - 232

4) 594
  - 133

5) 553
  - 333

6) 119
  - 101

7) 258
  - 137

8) 568
  - 137

9) 682
  - 150

10) 661
  - 651

11) 751
  - 241

12) 237
  - 104

13) 881
  - 801

14) 472
  - 400

15) 544
  - 501

16) 777
  - 226

17) 782
  - 512

18) 861
  - 531

19) 933
  - 912

20) 363
  - 222

21) 186
  - 105

22) 764
  - 413

23) 723
  - 303

24) 736
  - 420

25) 849
  - 243

Name _____

Triple Digit Subtraction - No Regrouping   Date _____

1) 453
  - 403

2) 554
  - 420

3) 513
  - 303

4) 296
  - 193

5) 963
  - 903

6) 452
  - 350

7) 885
  - 604

8) 968
  - 463

9) 164
  - 150

10) 663
  - 360

11) 312
  - 110

12) 589
  - 138

13) 558
  - 154

14) 944
  - 434

15) 383
  - 262

16) 725
  - 505

17) 455
  - 315

18) 819
  - 415

19) 421
  - 211

20) 445
  - 120

21) 873
  - 622

22) 453
  - 220

23) 427
  - 300

24) 433
  - 102

25) 933
  - 111

Name _____

Triple Digit Subtraction - No Regrouping   Date _____

1) 619
  − 411

2) 455
  − 225

3) 542
  − 220

4) 127
  − 112

5) 289
  − 164

6) 741
  − 120

7) 146
  − 120

8) 986
  − 472

9) 827
  − 121

10) 599
  − 193

11) 974
  − 553

12) 483
  − 451

13) 872
  − 130

14) 582
  − 511

15) 768
  − 162

16) 291
  − 231

17) 419
  − 100

18) 552
  − 211

19) 572
  − 160

20) 617
  − 515

21) 466
  − 103

22) 785
  − 625

23) 643
  − 413

24) 444
  − 232

25) 694
  − 353

Name _____

Triple Digit Subtraction - No Regrouping   Date _____

1) 275
  - 151

2) 544
  - 312

3) 725
  - 701

4) 583
  - 373

5) 979
  - 709

6) 136
  - 110

7) 351
  - 231

8) 781
  - 470

9) 529
  - 317

10) 537
  - 234

11) 343
  - 322

12) 633
  - 411

13) 925
  - 422

14) 226
  - 111

15) 225
  - 103

16) 243
  - 212

17) 466
  - 303

18) 695
  - 332

19) 881
  - 611

20) 845
  - 612

21) 871
  - 471

22) 652
  - 601

23) 897
  - 113

24) 446
  - 204

25) 825
  - 622

Name _____

Triple Digit Subtraction - No Regrouping   Date _____

1) 515
  - 311

2) 348
  - 312

3) 375
  - 331

4) 521
  - 400

5) 662
  - 212

6) 416
  - 301

7) 361
  - 320

8) 247
  - 232

9) 599
  - 153

10) 171
  - 141

11) 663
  - 331

12) 987
  - 754

13) 774
  - 540

14) 849
  - 623

15) 946
  - 521

16) 474
  - 300

17) 978
  - 800

18) 214
  - 201

19) 845
  - 310

20) 893
  - 611

21) 822
  - 412

22) 888
  - 188

23) 214
  - 203

24) 735
  - 605

25) 919
  - 703

Name _____

Triple Digit Subtraction - No Regrouping

Date _____

1)
$$
\begin{array}{r}
171 \\
- 161 \\
\hline
\end{array}
$$

2)
$$
\begin{array}{r}
762 \\
- 501 \\
\hline
\end{array}
$$

3)
$$
\begin{array}{r}
592 \\
- 500 \\
\hline
\end{array}
$$

4)
$$
\begin{array}{r}
351 \\
- 311 \\
\hline
\end{array}
$$

5)
$$
\begin{array}{r}
189 \\
- 179 \\
\hline
\end{array}
$$

6)
$$
\begin{array}{r}
468 \\
- 320 \\
\hline
\end{array}
$$

7)
$$
\begin{array}{r}
435 \\
- 324 \\
\hline
\end{array}
$$

8)
$$
\begin{array}{r}
872 \\
- 631 \\
\hline
\end{array}
$$

9)
$$
\begin{array}{r}
926 \\
- 211 \\
\hline
\end{array}
$$

10)
$$
\begin{array}{r}
425 \\
- 205 \\
\hline
\end{array}
$$

11)
$$
\begin{array}{r}
117 \\
- 112 \\
\hline
\end{array}
$$

12)
$$
\begin{array}{r}
755 \\
- 352 \\
\hline
\end{array}
$$

13)
$$
\begin{array}{r}
714 \\
- 602 \\
\hline
\end{array}
$$

14)
$$
\begin{array}{r}
296 \\
- 206 \\
\hline
\end{array}
$$

15)
$$
\begin{array}{r}
228 \\
- 202 \\
\hline
\end{array}
$$

16)
$$
\begin{array}{r}
184 \\
- 102 \\
\hline
\end{array}
$$

17)
$$
\begin{array}{r}
172 \\
- 130 \\
\hline
\end{array}
$$

18)
$$
\begin{array}{r}
886 \\
- 443 \\
\hline
\end{array}
$$

19)
$$
\begin{array}{r}
671 \\
- 520 \\
\hline
\end{array}
$$

20)
$$
\begin{array}{r}
165 \\
- 101 \\
\hline
\end{array}
$$

21)
$$
\begin{array}{r}
241 \\
- 140 \\
\hline
\end{array}
$$

22)
$$
\begin{array}{r}
182 \\
- 151 \\
\hline
\end{array}
$$

23)
$$
\begin{array}{r}
853 \\
- 843 \\
\hline
\end{array}
$$

24)
$$
\begin{array}{r}
413 \\
- 301 \\
\hline
\end{array}
$$

25)
$$
\begin{array}{r}
818 \\
- 105 \\
\hline
\end{array}
$$

Name _____

Date _____

Score /25

1) 928
  - 513

2) 466
  - 200

3) 565
  - 264

4) 154
  - 152

5) 771
  - 660

6) 688
  - 651

7) 579
  - 467

8) 422
  - 202

9) 919
  - 415

10) 866
   - 633

11) 743
   - 731

12) 232
   - 101

13) 995
   - 220

14) 612
   - 402

15) 841
   - 341

16) 656
   - 140

17) 432
   - 301

18) 544
   - 232

19) 948
   - 504

20) 817
   - 517

21) 438
   - 226

22) 858
   - 720

23) 678
   - 321

24) 644
   - 503

25) 843
   - 632

Name _____

Triple Digit Subtraction - Some Regrouping Date _____

1) 859
  - 420

2) 449
  - 440

3) 952
  - 748

4) 921
  - 915

5) 916
  - 719

6) 788
  - 331

7) 957
  - 955

8) 860
  - 600

9) 812
  - 130

10) 930
  - 130

11) 932
  - 528

12) 955
  - 949

13) 951
  - 935

14) 729
  - 691

15) 486
  - 102

16) 854
  - 105

17) 686
  - 359

18) 944
  - 691

19) 901
  - 151

20) 720
  - 656

21) 937
  - 894

22) 435
  - 363

23) 975
  - 875

24) 903
  - 881

25) 960
  - 859

DAY 72

Name _____

Score /25

Triple Digit Subtraction - Some Regrouping Date _____

1) 769
  - 728

2) 642
  - 515

3) 633
  - 561

4) 844
  - 755

5) 859
  - 819

6) 354
  - 313

7) 882
  - 465

8) 258
  - 243

9) 998
  - 147

10) 856
  - 676

11) 899
  - 826

12) 945
  - 868

13) 840
  - 256

14) 478
  - 452

15) 923
  - 511

16) 645
  - 258

17) 677
  - 383

18) 742
  - 183

19) 923
  - 873

20) 655
  - 500

21) 324
  - 152

22) 638
  - 404

23) 998
  - 990

24) 620
  - 207

25) 995
  - 739

Name _____

Triple Digit Subtraction - Some Regrouping   Date _____

1) 762
  - 531

2) 614
  - 583

3) 614
  - 408

4) 831
  - 525

5) 858
  - 546

6) 742
  - 684

7) 778
  - 417

8) 787
  - 174

9) 825
  - 375

10) 788
  - 293

11) 991
  - 823

12) 822
  - 688

13) 680
  - 384

14) 966
  - 667

15) 942
  - 918

16) 614
  - 579

17) 312
  - 310

18) 931
  - 563

19) 662
  - 500

20) 667
  - 638

21) 862
  - 619

22) 915
  - 710

23) 856
  - 830

24) 799
  - 315

25) 771
  - 336

Name _____

Triple Digit Subtraction - Some Regrouping   Date _____

1) 771
  - 646

2) 460
  - 199

3) 877
  - 853

4) 967
  - 772

5) 787
  - 491

6) 916
  - 369

7) 917
  - 411

8) 707
  - 656

9) 666
  - 306

10) 998
  - 701

11) 902
  - 707

12) 896
  - 783

13) 990
  - 967

14) 827
  - 709

15) 708
  - 241

16) 882
  - 723

17) 863
  - 375

18) 585
  - 542

19) 412
  - 188

20) 973
  - 806

21) 981
  - 926

22) 577
  - 170

23) 383
  - 377

24) 862
  - 696

25) 931
  - 414

Name _____

Triple Digit Subtraction - Some Regrouping Date _____

1)   738
  - 398

2)   721
  - 618

3)   548
  - 196

4)   195
  - 156

5)   821
  - 684

6)   925
  - 848

7)   880
  - 208

8)   538
  - 104

9)   930
  - 927

10)   959
   - 899

11)   471
   - 404

12)   743
   - 672

13)   363
   - 108

14)   486
   - 425

15)   983
   - 920

16)   922
   - 213

17)   984
   - 962

18)   900
   - 817

19)   993
   - 800

20)   993
   - 983

21)   925
   - 875

22)   613
   - 297

23)   250
   - 129

24)   774
   - 712

25)   684
   - 539

Name _____

Score /25

Triple Digit Subtraction - Some Regrouping   Date _____

1) $\begin{array}{r} 992 \\ -\ 913 \\ \hline \end{array}$
2) $\begin{array}{r} 907 \\ -\ 691 \\ \hline \end{array}$
3) $\begin{array}{r} 994 \\ -\ 892 \\ \hline \end{array}$
4) $\begin{array}{r} 695 \\ -\ 166 \\ \hline \end{array}$
5) $\begin{array}{r} 698 \\ -\ 506 \\ \hline \end{array}$

6) $\begin{array}{r} 857 \\ -\ 385 \\ \hline \end{array}$
7) $\begin{array}{r} 426 \\ -\ 352 \\ \hline \end{array}$
8) $\begin{array}{r} 753 \\ -\ 543 \\ \hline \end{array}$
9) $\begin{array}{r} 627 \\ -\ 466 \\ \hline \end{array}$
10) $\begin{array}{r} 914 \\ -\ 724 \\ \hline \end{array}$

11) $\begin{array}{r} 912 \\ -\ 847 \\ \hline \end{array}$
12) $\begin{array}{r} 227 \\ -\ 161 \\ \hline \end{array}$
13) $\begin{array}{r} 811 \\ -\ 129 \\ \hline \end{array}$
14) $\begin{array}{r} 805 \\ -\ 545 \\ \hline \end{array}$
15) $\begin{array}{r} 847 \\ -\ 193 \\ \hline \end{array}$

16) $\begin{array}{r} 998 \\ -\ 991 \\ \hline \end{array}$
17) $\begin{array}{r} 678 \\ -\ 357 \\ \hline \end{array}$
18) $\begin{array}{r} 687 \\ -\ 183 \\ \hline \end{array}$
19) $\begin{array}{r} 755 \\ -\ 158 \\ \hline \end{array}$
20) $\begin{array}{r} 338 \\ -\ 258 \\ \hline \end{array}$

21) $\begin{array}{r} 758 \\ -\ 704 \\ \hline \end{array}$
22) $\begin{array}{r} 765 \\ -\ 571 \\ \hline \end{array}$
23) $\begin{array}{r} 408 \\ -\ 340 \\ \hline \end{array}$
24) $\begin{array}{r} 781 \\ -\ 460 \\ \hline \end{array}$
25) $\begin{array}{r} 778 \\ -\ 636 \\ \hline \end{array}$

Name _____

Date _____

Score /25

1) 805
  - 711

2) 849
  - 528

3) 986
  - 953

4) 931
  - 835

5) 429
  - 242

6) 969
  - 938

7) 898
  - 376

8) 766
  - 664

9) 280
  - 249

10) 509
   - 390

11) 854
   - 804

12) 831
   - 672

13) 837
   - 729

14) 540
   - 532

15) 989
   - 979

16) 826
   - 123

17) 964
   - 928

18) 392
   - 297

19) 265
   - 182

20) 533
   - 393

21) 895
   - 826

22) 526
   - 210

23) 946
   - 868

24) 741
   - 145

25) 664
   - 599

DAY 78

Name _____

Score /25

Triple Digit Subtraction - Some Regrouping   Date _____

1) 944   2) 573   3) 915   4) 511   5) 918
 - 581   - 182   - 753   - 188   - 685

6) 740   7) 727   8) 898   9) 807   10) 560
 - 238   - 278   - 733   - 134   - 199

11) 936   12) 582   13) 771   14) 509   15) 626
  - 127   - 214   - 200   - 350   - 386

16) 941   17) 983   18) 567   19) 557   20) 680
  - 659   - 980   - 491   - 269   - 666

21) 840   22) 980   23) 863   24) 926   25) 742
  - 792   - 895   - 361   - 384   - 355

Name _____

Triple Digit Subtraction - Some Regrouping   Date _____

1) 854
  - 800

2) 944
  - 591

3) 774
  - 592

4) 991
  - 679

5) 781
  - 256

6) 924
  - 325

7) 354
  - 108

8) 792
  - 761

9) 928
  - 284

10) 991
   - 861

11) 458
   - 174

12) 830
   - 624

13) 615
   - 311

14) 989
   - 554

15) 960
   - 916

16) 997
   - 963

17) 945
   - 889

18) 364
   - 208

19) 982
   - 690

20) 648
   - 420

21) 954
   - 909

22) 617
   - 553

23) 827
   - 448

24) 758
   - 749

25) 826
   - 770

DAY 80

Score /25

Triple Digit Subtraction - Some Regrouping Date _____

1) 904
  - 472

2) 858
  - 758

3) 901
  - 302

4) 742
  - 202

5) 660
  - 117

6) 831
  - 477

7) 985
  - 964

8) 778
  - 703

9) 200
  - 147

10) 973
  - 104

11) 417
  - 219

12) 611
  - 395

13) 998
  - 233

14) 918
  - 566

15) 560
  - 385

16) 754
  - 678

17) 351
  - 327

18) 627
  - 527

19) 957
  - 832

20) 939
  - 684

21) 988
  - 322

22) 828
  - 778

23) 680
  - 108

24) 998
  - 995

25) 694
  - 237

Name _____

2-3 Digit Adding - Some Regrouping   Date _____

1)   449
   + 447

2)   263
   + 449

3)   957
   + 764

4)   596
   + 100

5)   863
   + 579

6)   830
   + 279

7)   239
   + 506

8)   97
   + 466

9)   998
   + 809

10)   921
    + 867

11)   329
    + 368

12)   261
    + 133

13)   958
    + 853

14)   272
    + 289

15)   61
    + 518

16)   805
    + 868

17)   938
    + 851

18)   85
    + 589

19)   845
    + 854

20)   651
    + 680

21)   909
    + 349

22)   533
    + 696

23)   454
    + 799

24)   758
    + 668

25)   79
    + 901

DAY 82

Name _____

2-3 Digit Subtraction - Some Regrouping Date _____

1) 804
  - 522

2) 755
  - 503

3) 396
  - 20

4) 978
  - 745

5) 863
  - 703

6) 208
  - 186

7) 306
  - 263

8) 818
  - 438

9) 671
  - 34

10) 534
   - 481

11) 435
   - 15

12) 301
   - 74

13) 145
   - 43

14) 957
   - 345

15) 653
   - 227

16) 442
   - 279

17) 319
   - 36

18) 988
   - 778

19) 394
   - 367

20) 505
   - 20

21) 358
   - 232

22) 197
   - 165

23) 306
   - 196

24) 656
   - 215

25) 965
   - 955

Name _____

2-3 Digit Adding - Some Regrouping

Date _____

1)   549
+ 764

2)   583
+ 973

3)   334
+ 707

4)   811
+ 154

5)   538
+ 721

6)   571
+ 441

7)   40
+ 194

8)   516
+ 578

9)   437
+ 981

10)   532
+ 170

11)   753
+ 873

12)   404
+ 638

13)   76
+ 541

14)   781
+ 400

15)   144
+ 329

16)   858
+ 947

17)   471
+ 273

18)   570
+ 160

19)   776
+ 555

20)   721
+ 307

21)   376
+ 574

22)   225
+ 74

23)   17
+ 867

24)   635
+ 739

25)   156
+ 216

Name _____

2-3 Digit Subtraction - Some Regrouping

Date _____

1) 808
  - 744

2) 62
  - 18

3) 145
  - 63

4) 157
  - 85

5) 155
  - 103

6) 164
  - 102

7) 589
  - 98

8) 504
  - 162

9) 386
  - 290

10) 950
  - 275

11) 457
  - 127

12) 322
  - 78

13) 275
  - 132

14) 878
  - 604

15) 136
  - 18

16) 800
  - 271

17) 919
  - 783

18) 171
  - 51

19) 602
  - 368

20) 173
  - 11

21) 961
  - 882

22) 311
  - 200

23) 367
  - 107

24) 944
  - 259

25) 475
  - 15

2-3 Digit Adding - Some Regrouping   Date _____

1) 862
  + 593

2) 327
  + 538

3) 936
  + 929

4) 808
  + 445

5) 370
  + 653

6) 413
  + 925

7) 545
  + 792

8) 413
  + 905

9) 519
  + 424

10) 445
  + 824

11) 807
  + 458

12) 425
  + 526

13) 983
  + 957

14)   15
  + 663

15) 790
  + 917

16) 101
  + 197

17) 768
  + 663

18) 882
  + 481

19)   85
  + 199

20) 185
  + 596

21) 836
  + 45

22) 911
  + 903

23) 463
  + 610

24) 465
  + 388

25)   13
  + 933

DAY 86

2-3 Digit Subtraction - Some Regrouping

Date _____

Score /25

1)
$$694 - 426$$

2)
$$880 - 159$$

3)
$$636 - 259$$

4)
$$275 - 88$$

5)
$$415 - 132$$

6)
$$846 - 14$$

7)
$$207 - 111$$

8)
$$195 - 146$$

9)
$$683 - 450$$

10)
$$898 - 412$$

11)
$$877 - 211$$

12)
$$373 - 70$$

13)
$$591 - 51$$

14)
$$749 - 123$$

15)
$$689 - 391$$

16)
$$824 - 161$$

17)
$$829 - 688$$

18)
$$655 - 161$$

19)
$$332 - 156$$

20)
$$316 - 16$$

21)
$$295 - 179$$

22)
$$372 - 131$$

23)
$$344 - 296$$

24)
$$683 - 27$$

25)
$$414 - 269$$

Name _____

Score /25

2-3 Digit Adding - Some Regrouping   Date _____

1) $596 + 562$

2) $314 + 120$

3) $422 + 902$

4) $35 + 876$

5) $705 + 100$

6) $421 + 679$

7) $685 + 246$

8) $498 + 229$

9) $587 + 830$

10) $900 + 866$

11) $428 + 602$

12) $738 + 299$

13) $574 + 63$

14) $365 + 500$

15) $931 + 449$

16) $485 + 872$

17) $922 + 69$

18) $117 + 878$

19) $558 + 238$

20) $62 + 61$

21) $375 + 711$

22) $965 + 74$

23) $173 + 923$

24) $501 + 133$

25) $657 + 345$

DAY 88

Name _____

2-3 Digit Subtraction - Some Regrouping

Date _____

1) 853
  − 577

2) 162
  − 88

3) 180
  − 55

4) 825
  − 770

5) 366
  − 304

6) 935
  − 311

7) 492
  − 400

8) 925
  − 582

9) 55
  − 38

10) 742
  − 406

11) 925
  − 457

12) 71
  − 16

13) 312
  − 249

14) 199
  − 37

15) 142
  − 118

16) 145
  − 61

17) 238
  − 111

18) 809
  − 397

19) 754
  − 718

20) 343
  − 187

21) 123
  − 16

22) 729
  − 698

23) 693
  − 630

24) 863
  − 119

25) 687
  − 431

Name _____

2-3 Digit Adding - Some Regrouping

Date _____

1) 639 + 12	2) 196 + 103	3) 18 + 704	4) 180 + 40	5) 99 + 711
6) 977 + 203	7) 608 + 563	8) 913 + 791	9) 48 + 288	10) 985 + 783
11) 297 + 164	12) 872 + 595	13) 272 + 407	14) 870 + 576	15) 180 + 436
16) 610 + 621	17) 549 + 689	18) 146 + 705	19) 237 + 180	20) 145 + 449
21) 980 + 950	22) 502 + 700	23) 390 + 925	24) 785 + 785	25) 959 + 436

Name _____

Score /25

2-3 Digit Subtraction - Some Regrouping   Date _____

1) 487
  - 140

2) 219
  - 173

3) 597
  - 502

4) 546
  - 341

5) 833
  - 239

6)   29
  - 17

7) 803
  - 408

8) 534
  - 479

9)   84
  - 57

10) 331
  - 107

11) 692
  - 565

12) 926
  - 670

13) 859
  - 299

14) 263
  - 186

15) 640
  - 22

16) 630
  - 308

17) 933
  - 290

18) 886
  - 848

19) 757
  - 664

20) 179
  - 86

21) 987
  - 597

22) 220
  - 209

23) 574
  - 367

24) 345
  - 196

25)   28
  - 12

Name _____

2-3 Digit Adding - Some Regrouping

Date _____

1) 130
  + 742

2) 918
  + 541

3) 445
  + 145

4)   41
  + 260

5) 301
  + 681

6) 985
  + 789

7) 474
  + 586

8) 318
  + 939

9) 154
  + 823

10) 516
  + 948

11) 840
  + 565

12) 742
  + 87

13) 129
  + 444

14) 409
  + 52

15)   45
  + 774

16)   58
  + 643

17) 798
  + 305

18) 616
  + 966

19) 968
  + 638

20) 550
  + 929

21) 228
  + 706

22) 431
  + 520

23)   43
  + 507

24) 700
  + 288

25) 442
  + 784

Name _____

2-3 Digit Subtraction - Some Regrouping

Date _____

1) 118
  $-\ 65$

2) 542
  $-\ 337$

3) 560
  $-\ 473$

4) 377
  $-\ 364$

5) 460
  $-\ 188$

6) 32
  $-\ 17$

7) 963
  $-\ 255$

8) 370
  $-\ 210$

9) 612
  $-\ 93$

10) 167
  $-\ 67$

11) 634
  $-\ 422$

12) 165
  $-\ 153$

13) 512
  $-\ 218$

14) 934
  $-\ 145$

15) 263
  $-\ 130$

16) 439
  $-\ 239$

17) 868
  $-\ 276$

18) 918
  $-\ 567$

19) 342
  $-\ 99$

20) 477
  $-\ 111$

21) 994
  $-\ 87$

22) 672
  $-\ 80$

23) 289
  $-\ 227$

24) 288
  $-\ 47$

25) 192
  $-\ 177$

Name _____

2-3 Digit Adding - Some Regrouping

Date _____

1) 191
  + 372

2) 470
  + 597

3) 652
  + 765

4) 504
  + 57

5) 274
  + 13

6) 810
  + 237

7) 444
  + 876

8) 410
  + 883

9)   21
  + 803

10) 288
  + 938

11) 301
  + 755

12) 501
  + 314

13) 622
  + 174

14)   48
  + 103

15) 185
  + 784

16) 515
  + 596

17) 789
  + 604

18)   21
  + 982

19) 705
  + 215

20)   69
  + 104

21) 463
  + 513

22) 722
  + 949

23) 321
  + 940

24) 785
  + 549

25) 410
  + 40

DAY 94

Name _____

2-3 Digit Subtraction - Some Regrouping

Date _____

1)
$$460 - 245$$

2)
$$847 - 143$$

3)
$$61 - 48$$

4)
$$721 - 454$$

5)
$$181 - 49$$

6)
$$661 - 552$$

7)
$$487 - 385$$

8)
$$661 - 143$$

9)
$$145 - 69$$

10)
$$321 - 13$$

11)
$$241 - 134$$

12)
$$465 - 264$$

13)
$$270 - 252$$

14)
$$916 - 442$$

15)
$$166 - 121$$

16)
$$945 - 27$$

17)
$$543 - 263$$

18)
$$86 - 12$$

19)
$$464 - 219$$

20)
$$622 - 542$$

21)
$$682 - 242$$

22)
$$752 - 278$$

23)
$$607 - 374$$

24)
$$411 - 198$$

25)
$$837 - 453$$

Name _____

2-3 Digit Adding - Some Regrouping

Date _____

1) 30
  + 857

2) 139
  + 280

3) 817
  + 18

4) 755
  + 322

5) 272
  + 996

6) 39
  + 42

7) 225
  + 582

8) 533
  + 265

9) 192
  + 526

10) 291
  + 325

11) 765
  + 801

12) 136
  + 245

13) 465
  + 999

14) 975
  + 213

15) 694
  + 728

16) 52
  + 62

17) 141
  + 210

18) 809
  + 159

19) 608
  + 554

20) 899
  + 109

21) 597
  + 547

22) 692
  + 43

23) 236
  + 384

24) 936
  + 751

25) 224
  + 360

DAY 96

2-3 Digit Subtraction - Some Regrouping

Date _____

Score /25

1) 998
  - 812

2) 243
  - 232

3) 314
  - 191

4) 613
  - 119

5) 556
  - 124

6) 521
  - 26

7) 426
  - 408

8) 627
  - 28

9) 904
  - 35

10) 137
   - 10

11) 557
   - 253

12) 191
   - 168

13) 342
   - 100

14) 700
   - 610

15) 320
   - 148

16) 576
   - 405

17) 618
   - 160

18) 479
   - 107

19) 490
   - 85

20)   85
   - 63

21) 313
   - 145

22) 873
   - 458

23) 221
   - 92

24) 705
   - 469

25) 760
   - 563

DAY 97

Name _____

Score /25

2-3 Digit Adding - Some Regrouping

Date _____

1) 599
  + 511

2) 979
  + 463

3) 356
  + 654

4) 382
  + 308

5) 673
  + 489

6) 237
  + 999

7) 697
  + 904

8) 890
  + 577

9) 170
  + 535

10) 82
  + 483

11) 418
  + 892

12) 904
  + 240

13) 662
  + 142

14) 436
  + 708

15) 113
  + 859

16) 293
  + 824

17) 796
  + 420

18) 755
  + 374

19) 669
  + 401

20) 130
  + 517

21) 987
  + 279

22) 118
  + 989

23) 335
  + 472

24) 530
  + 544

25) 557
  + 244

Name _____

2-3 Digit Subtraction - Some Regrouping

Date _____

1) $413 - 53$

2) $633 - 496$

3) $39 - 29$

4) $173 - 144$

5) $838 - 545$

6) $665 - 392$

7) $129 - 112$

8) $548 - 116$

9) $439 - 120$

10) $843 - 477$

11) $495 - 136$

12) $683 - 289$

13) $959 - 69$

14) $62 - 24$

15) $135 - 57$

16) $903 - 22$

17) $997 - 645$

18) $392 - 114$

19) $895 - 600$

20) $333 - 175$

21) $813 - 154$

22) $662 - 509$

23) $591 - 206$

24) $726 - 335$

25) $226 - 89$

DAY 99

Name _____

Score /25

2-3 Digit Adding - Some Regrouping   Date _____

1) 978
  + 749

2)   18
  + 162

3) 515
  + 411

4) 989
  + 315

5) 482
  + 520

6) 466
  + 243

7) 233
  + 94

8) 181
  + 671

9) 169
  + 64

10) 490
  + 885

11) 345
  + 685

12) 829
  + 765

13) 738
  + 482

14) 836
  + 871

15) 982
  + 45

16) 281
  + 573

17) 47
  + 542

18) 816
  + 475

19) 538
  + 546

20) 278
  + 675

21) 744
  + 119

22) 902
  + 550

23) 606
  + 105

24) 699
  + 933

25) 533
  + 690

99

DAY 100

Name _____

Score /25

2-3 Digit Subtraction - Some Regrouping

Date _____

1) 844
  - 615

2) 595
  - 489

3) 271
  - 232

4) 661
  - 577

5) 774
  - 581

6) 571
  - 514

7) 747
  - 494

8) 923
  - 437

9) 595
  - 248

10) 947
  - 923

11) 121
  - 27

12) 233
  - 23

13) 497
  - 177

14) 161
  - 111

15) 958
  - 873

16) 316
  - 73

17) 201
  - 51

18) 611
  - 440

19) 22
  - 12

20) 446
  - 298

21) 586
  - 192

22) 52
  - 35

23) 604
  - 105

24) 346
  - 329

25) 882
  - 169

ANSWER KEY

DAY 1
1) 48	2) 78	3) 95	4) 76	5) 77
6) 53	7) 77	8) 69	9) 48	10) 76
11) 63	12) 92	13) 99	14) 77	15) 56
16) 59	17) 58	18) 69	19) 98	20) 64
21) 38	22) 26	23) 55	24) 98	25) 68

DAY 2
1) 89	2) 59	3) 39	4) 49	5) 68
6) 76	7) 72	8) 58	9) 68	10) 74
11) 90	12) 85	13) 34	14) 92	15) 99
16) 94	17) 97	18) 68	19) 99	20) 69
21) 36	22) 75	23) 99	24) 69	25) 75

DAY 3
1) 78	2) 99	3) 73	4) 89	5) 59
6) 85	7) 89	8) 97	9) 59	10) 99
11) 95	12) 85	13) 73	14) 78	15) 99
16) 95	17) 71	18) 79	19) 97	20) 81
21) 89	22) 88	23) 89	24) 48	25) 25

DAY 4
1) 79	2) 39	3) 87	4) 98	5) 89
6) 90	7) 67	8) 98	9) 97	10) 56
11) 83	12) 93	13) 89	14) 77	15) 66
16) 91	17) 67	18) 99	19) 98	20) 73
21) 94	22) 46	23) 59	24) 56	25) 94

DAY 5
1) 83	2) 49	3) 75	4) 77	5) 89
6) 89	7) 49	8) 96	9) 79	10) 87
11) 63	12) 97	13) 98	14) 49	15) 95
16) 93	17) 95	18) 96	19) 98	20) 69
21) 99	22) 85	23) 97	24) 97	25) 92

DAY 6
1) 74	2) 89	3) 77	4) 98	5) 69
6) 96	7) 96	8) 98	9) 78	10) 92
11) 95	12) 89	13) 48	14) 98	15) 89
16) 94	17) 89	18) 86	19) 88	20) 75
21) 59	22) 98	23) 59	24) 88	25) 24

DAY 7
1) 92	2) 89	3) 29	4) 77	5) 86
6) 88	7) 97	8) 87	9) 39	10) 78
11) 94	12) 99	13) 39	14) 99	15) 73
16) 86	17) 76	18) 87	19) 57	20) 49
21) 99	22) 98	23) 98	24) 88	25) 93

DAY 8
1) 58	2) 89	3) 76	4) 58	5) 98
6) 99	7) 89	8) 58	9) 29	10) 77
11) 98	12) 95	13) 79	14) 94	15) 89
16) 98	17) 77	18) 89	19) 99	20) 59
21) 69	22) 99	23) 99	24) 68	25) 96

DAY 9
1) 46	2) 97	3) 75	4) 86	5) 94
6) 85	7) 79	8) 96	9) 49	10) 97
11) 69	12) 75	13) 93	14) 80	15) 74
16) 58	17) 76	18) 48	19) 85	20) 45
21) 91	22) 59	23) 29	24) 69	25) 59

DAY 10
1) 55	2) 65	3) 89	4) 69	5) 98
6) 89	7) 68	8) 87	9) 95	10) 89
11) 67	12) 39	13) 68	14) 92	15) 96
16) 92	17) 38	18) 96	19) 50	20) 57
21) 97	22) 95	23) 69	24) 94	25) 89

DAY 11
1) 75	2) 77	3) 70	4) 36	5) 84
6) 109	7) 58	8) 146	9) 103	10) 103
11) 67	12) 80	13) 173	14) 72	15) 37
16) 99	17) 137	18) 128	19) 102	20) 155
21) 143	22) 131	23) 156	24) 163	25) 92

DAY 12
1) 144	2) 121	3) 129	4) 85	5) 68
6) 101	7) 138	8) 60	9) 172	10) 68
11) 124	12) 86	13) 111	14) 96	15) 101
16) 78	17) 140	18) 129	19) 131	20) 109
21) 101	22) 44	23) 111	24) 142	25) 134

DAY 13
1) 117	2) 89	3) 153	4) 94	5) 144
6) 24	7) 114	8) 33	9) 87	10) 81
11) 114	12) 101	13) 84	14) 117	15) 110
16) 108	17) 126	18) 87	19) 121	20) 118
21) 118	22) 112	23) 118	24) 66	25) 77

DAY 14
1) 112	2) 99	3) 156	4) 86	5) 112
6) 166	7) 154	8) 60	9) 145	10) 151
11) 72	12) 101	13) 163	14) 41	15) 146
16) 76	17) 121	18) 156	19) 148	20) 109
21) 38	22) 110	23) 21	24) 130	25) 108

DAY 15
1) 95	2) 113	3) 138	4) 98	5) 67
6) 110	7) 120	8) 79	9) 150	10) 120
11) 72	12) 129	13) 96	14) 159	15) 47
16) 26	17) 130	18) 99	19) 74	20) 74
21) 134	22) 83	23) 65	24) 64	25) 100

ANSWER KEY

DAY 16
1) 104	2) 150	3) 103	4) 28	5) 131
6) 167	7) 114	8) 68	9) 101	10) 99
11) 143	12) 92	13) 150	14) 48	15) 64
16) 98	17) 68	18) 127	19) 150	20) 93
21) 59	22) 111	23) 59	24) 62	25) 119

DAY 17
1) 89	2) 97	3) 99	4) 135	5) 92
6) 70	7) 122	8) 128	9) 94	10) 186
11) 146	12) 57	13) 122	14) 26	15) 75
16) 145	17) 100	18) 124	19) 114	20) 119
21) 136	22) 140	23) 21	24) 113	25) 83

DAY 18
1) 70	2) 124	3) 74	4) 149	5) 89
6) 161	7) 23	8) 104	9) 98	10) 84
11) 140	12) 90	13) 95	14) 84	15) 94
16) 116	17) 61	18) 159	19) 156	20) 15
21) 74	22) 52	23) 78	24) 82	25) 12

DAY 19
1) 105	2) 98	3) 61	4) 46	5) 106
6) 126	7) 118	8) 125	9) 88	10) 134
11) 57	12) 106	13) 81	14) 126	15) 132
16) 152	17) 115	18) 110	19) 116	20) 144
21) 150	22) 127	23) 56	24) 78	25) 110

DAY 20
1) 147	2) 135	3) 131	4) 149	5) 113
6) 142	7) 142	8) 157	9) 124	10) 78
11) 102	12) 92	13) 36	14) 119	15) 146
16) 106	17) 128	18) 171	19) 85	20) 95
21) 54	22) 130	23) 47	24) 56	25) 112

DAY 21
1) 967	2) 897	3) 859	4) 976	5) 88
6) 995	7) 787	8) 888	9) 888	10) 95
11) 895	12) 979	13) 985	14) 627	15) 84
16) 879	17) 564	18) 995	19) 732	20) 75
21) 956	22) 568	23) 868	24) 579	25) 57

DAY 22
1) 499	2) 435	3) 483	4) 462	5) 587
6) 999	7) 673	8) 765	9) 757	10) 724
11) 639	12) 698	13) 667	14) 954	15) 674
16) 787	17) 758	18) 869	19) 977	20) 788
21) 661	22) 967	23) 896	24) 989	25) 875

DAY 23
1) 437	2) 579	3) 683	4) 883	5) 788
6) 884	7) 887	8) 668	9) 969	10) 489
11) 998	12) 953	13) 419	14) 787	15) 454
16) 998	17) 996	18) 648	19) 566	20) 796
21) 894	22) 880	23) 933	24) 667	25) 988

DAY 24
1) 389	2) 786	3) 791	4) 865	5) 82
6) 445	7) 975	8) 552	9) 962	10) 38
11) 837	12) 959	13) 915	14) 656	15) 69
16) 659	17) 897	18) 589	19) 594	20) 31
21) 878	22) 995	23) 929	24) 665	25) 95

DAY 25
1) 498	2) 851	3) 789	4) 698	5) 585
6) 787	7) 679	8) 887	9) 585	10) 854
11) 626	12) 999	13) 939	14) 676	15) 465
16) 898	17) 898	18) 999	19) 397	20) 996
21) 989	22) 399	23) 995	24) 899	25) 929

DAY 26
1) 838	2) 779	3) 937	4) 978	5) 887
6) 842	7) 696	8) 892	9) 859	10) 979
11) 995	12) 958	13) 958	14) 485	15) 937
16) 965	17) 399	18) 972	19) 938	20) 628
21) 766	22) 799	23) 989	24) 949	25) 986

DAY 27
1) 397	2) 757	3) 979	4) 338	5) 97
6) 629	7) 729	8) 799	9) 946	10) 61
11) 968	12) 658	13) 793	14) 987	15) 86
16) 997	17) 795	18) 479	19) 769	20) 88
21) 746	22) 477	23) 879	24) 999	25) 33

DAY 28
1) 998	2) 999	3) 669	4) 397	5) 698
6) 779	7) 788	8) 449	9) 889	10) 999
11) 398	12) 269	13) 948	14) 579	15) 935
16) 491	17) 538	18) 949	19) 796	20) 847
21) 899	22) 994	23) 975	24) 934	25) 475

DAY 29
1) 769	2) 976	3) 829	4) 587	5) 758
6) 848	7) 901	8) 897	9) 678	10) 948
11) 976	12) 939	13) 278	14) 639	15) 498
16) 679	17) 856	18) 249	19) 589	20) 754
21) 576	22) 989	23) 894	24) 969	25) 819

DAY 30
1) 997	2) 578	3) 949	4) 979	5) 89
6) 577	7) 798	8) 968	9) 797	10) 67
11) 894	12) 889	13) 643	14) 989	15) 49
16) 788	17) 757	18) 724	19) 668	20) 77
21) 817	22) 797	23) 341	24) 968	25) 81

DAY 31

1) 343　2) 1676　3) 749　4) 1710　5) 712

6) 1199　7) 1327　8) 1315　9) 1208　10) 611

11) 1257　12) 1265　13) 876　14) 1074　15) 1222

16) 1296　17) 1708　18) 1286　19) 765　20) 1702

21) 467　22) 1123　23) 535　24) 1251　25) 708

DAY 32

1) 1252　2) 1008　3) 471　4) 770　5) 1210

6) 428　7) 729　8) 1041　9) 833　10) 591

11) 1542　12) 606　13) 1328　14) 1478　15) 1219

16) 1761　17) 1235　18) 1460　19) 1741　20) 1060

21) 760　22) 1097　23) 1134　24) 1157　25) 1476

DAY 33

1) 1278　2) 984　3) 1321　4) 1080　5) 1536

6) 1608　7) 810　8) 1196　9) 671　10) 1302

11) 633　12) 1566　13) 1192　14) 553　15) 880

16) 989　17) 1420　18) 1070　19) 1455　20) 877

21) 760　22) 1143　23) 891　24) 1265　25) 1699

DAY 34

1) 1340　2) 723　3) 1118　4) 1120　5) 835

6) 1233　7) 1080　8) 1101　9) 1279　10) 1091

11) 407　12) 457　13) 1572　14) 1231　15) 1506

16) 271　17) 922　18) 1778　19) 953　20) 619

21) 1641　22) 678　23) 1546　24) 1289　25) 554

DAY 35

1) 1553　2) 370　3) 1657　4) 524　5) 496

6) 938　7) 928　8) 1640　9) 1325　10) 942

11) 1203　12) 1422　13) 897　14) 908　15) 1402

16) 606　17) 391　18) 925　19) 714　20) 1443

21) 540　22) 1222　23) 1868　24) 907　25) 1183

DAY 36

1) 1931　2) 828　3) 1708　4) 1050　5) 1364

6) 790　7) 1471　8) 1250　9) 1690　10) 1413

11) 1536　12) 757　13) 964　14) 1837　15) 1217

16) 1049　17) 1348　18) 1149　19) 1256　20) 1356

21) 1274　22) 1078　23) 1093　24) 453　25) 600

DAY 37

1) 1044　2) 1256　3) 1452　4) 1286　5) 1115

6) 1640　7) 889　8) 1294　9) 1573　10) 1472

11) 911　12) 952　13) 745　14) 1255　15) 847

16) 542　17) 645　18) 1279　19) 1314　20) 1736

21) 708　22) 1331　23) 1803　24) 1335　25) 1462

DAY 38

1) 690　2) 1254　3) 950　4) 1231　5) 1612

6) 1242　7) 1173　8) 1394　9) 1819　10) 1036

11) 952　12) 1601　13) 799　14) 1322　15) 1083

16) 385　17) 1336　18) 876　19) 1237　20) 1605

21) 1225　22) 794　23) 636　24) 1373　25) 1422

DAY 39

1) 1303　2) 414　3) 1110　4) 1159　5) 1361

6) 1038　7) 542　8) 1127　9) 1018　10) 833

11) 1926　12) 1253　13) 305　14) 861　15) 718

16) 1631　17) 1487　18) 1441　19) 238　20) 657

21) 958　22) 1020　23) 804　24) 1321　25) 1091

DAY 40

1) 836　2) 1208　3) 1078　4) 1354　5) 1483

6) 1876　7) 921　8) 1751　9) 1594　10) 1798

11) 1741　12) 1129　13) 1569　14) 1806　15) 1196

16) 1173　17) 943　18) 1170　19) 1408　20) 1475

21) 715　22) 738　23) 1623　24) 1337　25) 934

DAY 41

1) 4　2) 11　3) 11　4) 10　5) 42

6) 42　7) 11　8) 4　9) 7　10) 80

11) 3　12) 83　13) 11　14) 11　15) 10

16) 13　17) 27　18) 21　19) 81　20) 14

21) 28　22) 5　23) 51　24) 22　25) 5

DAY 42

1) 44　2) 11　3) 35　4) 50　5) 23

6) 14　7) 14　8) 15　9) 10　10) 15

11) 35　12) 11　13) 30　14) 40　15) 31

16) 21　17) 62　18) 76　19) 81　20) 30

21) 65　22) 20　23) 65　24) 16　25) 57

DAY 43

1) 13　2) 1　3) 50　4) 12　5) 41

6) 43　7) 41　8) 11　9) 8　10) 17

11) 44　12) 70　13) 20　14) 10　15) 61

16) 44　17) 22　18) 51　19) 20　20) 10

21) 62　22) 20　23) 2　24) 21　25) 20

DAY 44

1) 17　2) 65　3) 3　4) 10　5) 50

6) 53　7) 3　8) 62　9) 16　10) 25

11) 54　12) 3　13) 21　14) 13　15) 47

16) 61　17) 30　18) 2　19) 4　20) 31

21) 12　22) 76　23) 12　24) 23　25) 21

DAY 45

1) 41　2) 24　3) 60　4) 45　5) 2

6) 31　7) 3　8) 50　9) 23　10) 41

11) 3　12) 8　13) 28　14) 10　15) 41

16) 12　17) 2　18) 15　19) 2　20) 10

21) 21　22) 31　23) 51　24) 23　25) 21

ANSWER KEY

DAY 46
1) 0	2) 6	3) 41	4) 32	5) 50
6) 52	7) 43	8) 10	9) 14	10) 53
11) 2	12) 42	13) 34	14) 25	15) 82
16) 21	17) 22	18) 31	19) 3	20) 11
21) 8	22) 52	23) 83	24) 20	25) 23

DAY 47
1) 17	2) 31	3) 7	4) 41	5) 21
6) 17	7) 18	8) 32	9) 43	10) 22
11) 50	12) 14	13) 10	14) 26	15) 20
16) 12	17) 11	18) 13	19) 12	20) 42
21) 2	22) 67	23) 40	24) 45	25) 13

DAY 48
1) 61	2) 42	3) 37	4) 40	5) 45
6) 12	7) 50	8) 27	9) 40	10) 26
11) 82	12) 51	13) 10	14) 62	15) 22
16) 21	17) 11	18) 19	19) 71	20) 38
21) 20	22) 61	23) 14	24) 61	25) 12

DAY 49
1) 20	2) 20	3) 11	4) 30	5) 4
6) 13	7) 26	8) 44	9) 10	10) 61
11) 14	12) 42	13) 50	14) 54	15) 3
16) 4	17) 83	18) 23	19) 62	20) 21
21) 5	22) 14	23) 41	24) 33	25) 20

DAY 50
1) 10	2) 56	3) 1	4) 23	5) 10
6) 16	7) 4	8) 73	9) 11	10) 12
11) 8	12) 3	13) 30	14) 51	15) 30
16) 40	17) 12	18) 24	19) 72	20) 61
21) 4	22) 12	23) 20	24) 41	25) 3

DAY 51
1) 59	2) 42	3) 58	4) 22	5) 2
6) 71	7) 42	8) 2	9) 59	10) 1
11) 23	12) 22	13) 49	14) 16	15)
16) 16	17) 3	18) 2	19) 38	20)
21) 6	22) 16	23) 38	24) 4	25)

DAY 52
1) 42	2) 7	3) 5	4) 46	5) 36
6) 3	7) 15	8) 43	9) 9	10) 18
11) 66	12) 49	13) 44	14) 19	15) 25
16) 22	17) 83	18) 2	19) 7	20) 36
21) 32	22) 58	23) 49	24) 11	25) 13

DAY 53
1) 4	2) 13	3) 66	4) 19	5) 69
6) 19	7) 7	8) 63	9) 27	10) 43
11) 28	12) 37	13) 69	14) 75	15) 20
16) 22	17) 29	18) 16	19) 53	20) 12
21) 23	22) 66	23) 45	24) 37	25) 26

DAY 54
1) 32	2) 22	3) 7	4) 11	5) 3
6) 11	7) 18	8) 4	9) 30	10) 4
11) 17	12) 5	13) 18	14) 33	15)
16) 54	17) 25	18) 4	19) 28	20) 4
21) 3	22) 10	23) 26	24) 34	25) 4

DAY 55
1) 6	2) 18	3) 4	4) 19	5) 14
6) 33	7) 39	8) 40	9) 50	10) 4
11) 15	12) 45	13) 6	14) 3	15) 38
16) 71	17) 47	18) 26	19) 60	20) 36
21) 12	22) 10	23) 14	24) 5	25) 11

DAY 56
1) 16	2) 9	3) 56	4) 4	5) 13
6) 6	7) 32	8) 38	9) 22	10) 74
11) 11	12) 4	13) 58	14) 15	15) 76
16) 18	17) 58	18) 80	19) 14	20) 73
21) 6	22) 37	23) 72	24) 72	25) 28

DAY 57
1) 43	2) 2	3) 22	4) 49	5)
6) 55	7) 48	8) 10	9) 32	10) 2
11) 4	12) 25	13) 55	14) 42	15) 6
16) 14	17) 6	18) 33	19) 42	20)
21) 4	22) 13	23) 18	24) 4	25) 7

DAY 58
1) 9	2) 49	3) 8	4) 3	5) 13
6) 64	7) 73	8) 5	9) 40	10) 4
11) 14	12) 35	13) 8	14) 26	15) 4
16) 37	17) 18	18) 26	19) 12	20) 32
21) 15	22) 6	23) 21	24) 17	25) 16

DAY 59
1) 4	2) 61	3) 4	4) 17	5) 25
6) 72	7) 6	8) 46	9) 15	10) 2
11) 17	12) 24	13) 22	14) 33	15) 14
16) 13	17) 38	18) 22	19) 20	20) 57
21) 11	22) 12	23) 8	24) 44	25) 44

DAY 60
1) 39	2) 24	3) 10	4) 7	5)
6) 3	7) 11	8) 27	9) 3	10) 4
11) 26	12) 7	13) 2	14) 25	15) 6
16) 29	17) 25	18) 10	19) 11	20) 3
21) 16	22) 55	23) 5	24) 21	25) 2

ANSWER KEY

DAY 61

1) 33 2) 10 3) 529 4) 814 5) 194
6) 166 7) 511 8) 31 9) 115 10) 222
11) 51 12) 24 13) 48 14) 161 15) 104
16) 11 17) 301 18) 133 19) 618 20) 24
21) 540 22) 481 23) 211 24) 183 25) 520

DAY 62

1) 252 2) 110 3) 230 4) 140 5) 154
6) 565 7) 270 8) 207 9) 410 10) 127
11) 98 12) 210 13) 335 14) 506 15) 30
16) 200 17) 21 18) 101 19) 200 20) 645
21) 60 22) 428 23) 17 24) 114 25) 244

DAY 63

1) 413 2) 2 3) 253 4) 476 5) 114
6) 113 7) 15 8) 110 9) 502 10) 413
11) 112 12) 503 13) 21 14) 111 15) 742
16) 400 17) 151 18) 113 19) 410 20) 131
21) 120 22) 432 23) 152 24) 15 25) 161

DAY 64

1) 421 2) 232 3) 120 4) 461 5) 220
6) 18 7) 121 8) 431 9) 532 10) 10
11) 510 12) 133 13) 80 14) 72 15) 43
16) 551 17) 270 18) 330 19) 21 20) 141
21) 81 22) 351 23) 420 24) 316 25) 606

DAY 65

1) 50 2) 134 3) 210 4) 103 5) 60
6) 102 7) 281 8) 505 9) 14 10) 303
11) 202 12) 451 13) 404 14) 510 15) 121
16) 220 17) 140 18) 404 19) 210 20) 325
21) 251 22) 233 23) 127 24) 331 25) 822

DAY 66

1) 208 2) 230 3) 322 4) 15 5) 125
6) 621 7) 26 8) 514 9) 706 10) 406
11) 421 12) 32 13) 742 14) 71 15) 606
16) 60 17) 319 18) 341 19) 412 20) 102
21) 363 22) 160 23) 230 24) 212 25) 341

DAY 67

1) 124 2) 232 3) 24 4) 210 5) 270
6) 26 7) 120 8) 311 9) 212 10) 303
11) 21 12) 222 13) 503 14) 115 15) 122
16) 31 17) 163 18) 363 19) 270 20) 233
21) 400 22) 51 23) 784 24) 242 25) 203

DAY 68

1) 204 2) 36 3) 44 4) 121 5) 450
6) 115 7) 41 8) 15 9) 446 10) 30
11) 332 12) 233 13) 234 14) 226 15) 425
16) 174 17) 178 18) 13 19) 535 20) 282
21) 410 22) 700 23) 11 24) 130 25) 216

DAY 69

1) 10 2) 261 3) 92 4) 40 5) 10
6) 148 7) 111 8) 241 9) 715 10) 220
11) 5 12) 403 13) 112 14) 90 15) 26
16) 82 17) 42 18) 443 19) 151 20) 64
21) 101 22) 31 23) 10 24) 112 25) 713

DAY 70

1) 415 2) 266 3) 301 4) 2 5) 111
6) 37 7) 112 8) 220 9) 504 10) 233
11) 12 12) 131 13) 775 14) 210 15) 500
16) 516 17) 131 18) 312 19) 444 20) 300
21) 212 22) 138 23) 357 24) 141 25) 211

DAY 71

1) 439 2) 9 3) 204 4) 6 5) 197
6) 457 7) 2 8) 260 9) 682 10) 800
11) 404 12) 6 13) 16 14) 38 15) 384
16) 749 17) 327 18) 253 19) 750 20) 64
21) 43 22) 72 23) 100 24) 22 25) 101

DAY 72

1) 41 2) 127 3) 72 4) 89 5) 40
6) 41 7) 417 8) 15 9) 851 10) 180
11) 73 12) 77 13) 584 14) 26 15) 412
16) 387 17) 294 18) 559 19) 50 20) 155
21) 172 22) 234 23) 8 24) 413 25) 256

DAY 73

1) 231 2) 31 3) 206 4) 306 5) 312
6) 58 7) 361 8) 613 9) 450 10) 495
11) 168 12) 134 13) 296 14) 299 15) 24
16) 35 17) 2 18) 368 19) 162 20) 29
21) 243 22) 205 23) 26 24) 484 25) 435

DAY 74

1) 125 2) 261 3) 24 4) 195 5) 296
6) 547 7) 506 8) 51 9) 360 10) 297
11) 195 12) 113 13) 23 14) 118 15) 467
16) 159 17) 488 18) 43 19) 224 20) 167
21) 55 22) 407 23) 6 24) 166 25) 517

DAY 75

1) 340 2) 103 3) 352 4) 39 5) 137
6) 77 7) 672 8) 434 9) 3 10) 60
11) 67 12) 71 13) 255 14) 61 15) 63
16) 709 17) 22 18) 83 19) 193 20) 10
21) 50 22) 316 23) 121 24) 62 25) 145

DAY 76
1) 79 2) 216 3) 102 4) 529 5) 192
6) 472 7) 74 8) 210 9) 161 10) 190
11) 65 12) 66 13) 682 14) 260 15) 654
16) 7 17) 321 18) 504 19) 597 20) 80
21) 54 22) 194 23) 68 24) 321 25) 142

DAY 77
1) 94 2) 321 3) 33 4) 96 5) 187
6) 31 7) 522 8) 102 9) 31 10) 119
11) 50 12) 159 13) 108 14) 8 15) 10
16) 703 17) 36 18) 95 19) 83 20) 140
21) 69 22) 316 23) 78 24) 596 25) 65

DAY 78
1) 363 2) 391 3) 162 4) 323 5) 233
6) 502 7) 449 8) 165 9) 673 10) 361
11) 809 12) 368 13) 571 14) 159 15) 240
16) 282 17) 3 18) 76 19) 288 20) 14
21) 48 22) 85 23) 502 24) 542 25) 387

DAY 79
1) 54 2) 353 3) 182 4) 312 5) 525
6) 599 7) 246 8) 31 9) 644 10) 130
11) 284 12) 206 13) 304 14) 435 15) 44
16) 34 17) 56 18) 156 19) 292 20) 228
21) 45 22) 64 23) 379 24) 9 25) 56

DAY 80
1) 432 2) 100 3) 599 4) 540 5) 543
6) 354 7) 21 8) 75 9) 53 10) 869
11) 198 12) 216 13) 765 14) 352 15) 175
16) 76 17) 24 18) 100 19) 125 20) 255
21) 666 22) 50 23) 572 24) 3 25) 457

DAY 81
1) 896 2) 712 3) 1721 4) 696 5) 1442
6) 1109 7) 745 8) 563 9) 1807 10) 1788
11) 697 12) 394 13) 1811 14) 561 15) 579
16) 1673 17) 1789 18) 674 19) 1699 20) 1331
21) 1258 22) 1229 23) 1253 24) 1426 25) 980

DAY 82
1) 282 2) 252 3) 376 4) 233 5) 160
6) 22 7) 43 8) 380 9) 637 10) 53
11) 420 12) 227 13) 102 14) 612 15) 426
16) 163 17) 283 18) 210 19) 27 20) 485
21) 126 22) 32 23) 110 24) 441 25) 10

DAY 83
1) 1313 2) 1556 3) 1041 4) 965 5) 1259
6) 1012 7) 234 8) 1094 9) 1418 10) 702
11) 1626 12) 1042 13) 617 14) 1181 15) 473
16) 1805 17) 744 18) 730 19) 1331 20) 1028
21) 950 22) 299 23) 884 24) 1374 25) 372

DAY 84
1) 64 2) 44 3) 82 4) 72 5) 52
6) 62 7) 491 8) 342 9) 96 10) 675
11) 330 12) 244 13) 143 14) 274 15) 11
16) 529 17) 136 18) 120 19) 234 20) 163
21) 79 22) 111 23) 260 24) 685 25) 46

DAY 85
1) 1455 2) 865 3) 1865 4) 1253 5) 1023
6) 1338 7) 1337 8) 1318 9) 943 10) 1269
11) 1265 12) 951 13) 1940 14) 678 15) 1707
16) 298 17) 1431 18) 1363 19) 284 20) 781
21) 881 22) 1814 23) 1073 24) 853 25) 946

DAY 86
1) 268 2) 721 3) 377 4) 187 5) 283
6) 832 7) 96 8) 49 9) 233 10) 486
11) 666 12) 303 13) 540 14) 626 15) 298
16) 663 17) 141 18) 494 19) 176 20) 300
21) 116 22) 241 23) 48 24) 656 25) 145

DAY 87
1) 1158 2) 434 3) 1324 4) 911 5) 80
6) 1100 7) 931 8) 727 9) 1417 10) 176
11) 1030 12) 1037 13) 637 14) 865 15) 138
16) 1357 17) 991 18) 995 19) 796 20) 12
21) 1086 22) 1039 23) 1096 24) 634 25) 100

DAY 88
1) 276 2) 74 3) 125 4) 55 5) 62
6) 624 7) 92 8) 343 9) 17 10) 336
11) 468 12) 55 13) 63 14) 162 15) 24
16) 84 17) 127 18) 412 19) 36 20) 156
21) 107 22) 31 23) 63 24) 744 25) 256

DAY 89
1) 651 2) 299 3) 722 4) 220 5) 810
6) 1180 7) 1171 8) 1704 9) 336 10) 1768
11) 461 12) 1467 13) 679 14) 1446 15) 616
16) 1231 17) 1238 18) 851 19) 417 20) 594
21) 1930 22) 1202 23) 1315 24) 1570 25) 1395

DAY 90
1) 347 2) 46 3) 95 4) 205 5) 59
6) 12 7) 395 8) 55 9) 27 10) 22
11) 127 12) 256 13) 560 14) 77 15) 61
16) 322 17) 643 18) 38 19) 93 20) 9
21) 390 22) 11 23) 207 24) 149 25) 1

ANSWER KEY

DAY 91

1) 872	2) 1459	3) 590	4) 301	5) 982
6) 1774	7) 1060	8) 1257	9) 977	10) 1464
11) 1405	12) 829	13) 573	14) 461	15) 819
16) 701	17) 1103	18) 1582	19) 1606	20) 1479
21) 934	22) 951	23) 550	24) 988	25) 1226

DAY 92

1) 53	2) 205	3) 87	4) 13	5) 272
6) 15	7) 708	8) 160	9) 519	10) 100
11) 212	12) 12	13) 294	14) 789	15) 133
16) 200	17) 592	18) 351	19) 243	20) 366
21) 907	22) 592	23) 62	24) 241	25) 15

DAY 93

1) 563	2) 1067	3) 1417	4) 561	5) 287
6) 1047	7) 1320	8) 1293	9) 824	10) 1226
11) 1056	12) 815	13) 796	14) 151	15) 969
16) 1111	17) 1393	18) 1003	19) 920	20) 173
21) 976	22) 1671	23) 1261	24) 1334	25) 450

DAY 94

1) 215	2) 704	3) 13	4) 267	5) 132
6) 109	7) 102	8) 518	9) 76	10) 308
11) 107	12) 201	13) 18	14) 474	15) 45
16) 918	17) 280	18) 74	19) 245	20) 80
21) 440	22) 474	23) 233	24) 213	25) 384

DAY 95

1) 887	2) 419	3) 835	4) 1077	5) 1268
6) 81	7) 807	8) 798	9) 718	10) 616
11) 1566	12) 381	13) 1464	14) 1188	15) 1422
16) 114	17) 351	18) 968	19) 1162	20) 1008
21) 1144	22) 735	23) 620	24) 1687	25) 584

DAY 96

1) 186	2) 11	3) 123	4) 494	5) 432
6) 495	7) 18	8) 599	9) 869	10) 127
11) 304	12) 23	13) 242	14) 90	15) 172
16) 171	17) 458	18) 372	19) 405	20) 22
21) 168	22) 415	23) 129	24) 236	25) 197

DAY 97

1) 1110	2) 1442	3) 1010	4) 690	5) 1162
6) 1236	7) 1601	8) 1467	9) 705	10) 565
11) 1310	12) 1144	13) 804	14) 1144	15) 972
16) 1117	17) 1216	18) 1129	19) 1070	20) 647
21) 1266	22) 1107	23) 807	24) 1074	25) 801

DAY 98

1) 360	2) 137	3) 10	4) 29	5) 293
6) 273	7) 17	8) 432	9) 319	10) 366
11) 359	12) 394	13) 890	14) 38	15) 78
16) 881	17) 352	18) 278	19) 295	20) 158
21) 659	22) 153	23) 385	24) 391	25) 137

DAY 99

1) 1727	2) 180	3) 926	4) 1304	5) 1002
6) 709	7) 327	8) 852	9) 233	10) 1375
11) 1030	12) 1594	13) 1220	14) 1707	15) 1027
16) 854	17) 589	18) 1291	19) 1084	20) 953
21) 863	22) 1452	23) 711	24) 1632	25) 1223

DAY 100

1) 229	2) 106	3) 39	4) 84	5) 193
6) 57	7) 253	8) 486	9) 347	10) 24
11) 94	12) 210	13) 320	14) 50	15) 85
16) 243	17) 150	18) 171	19) 10	20) 148
21) 394	22) 17	23) 499	24) 17	25) 713

Made in the USA
Columbia, SC
08 April 2024

34108641R00061